THE BODY

LH Oppenheimer 1952

STUDIES IN BIBLICAL THEOLOGY

THE BODY

A Study in
Pauline Theology

JOHN A. T. ROBINSON

SCM PRESS LTD
56 BLOOMSBURY STREET
LONDON

First published 1952

Printed in Great Britain by
Robert Cunningham and Sons Ltd., Alva

CONTENTS

INTRODUCTION

THIS book is written from two basic convictions.

The first has to do with the significance of the mass man for the understanding of our situation and for the presentation of the Gospel to it. It has presumably always been true that 'even strong personalities are sixty to eighty per cent the result of environment, about twenty to forty per cent representing their personal contribution. Feeble personalities—the masses—are ninety to ninety-nine per cent their environment' (*France Pagan?*, ed. M. Ward, 77). But to-day we are faced with a position where the effect of every pressure, conscious and much more unconscious, is to strengthen the communal and correspondingly to weaken the individual forces in the personal equilibrium. The age of individualism is over, and with it its aim of social salvation as independence (economic, political and religious) from responsibility to and dominance by the authority of the group. Such an ideal is now no longer an economic possibility, though there are still those who wish it were politically or religiously attainable. The basic economic fact of our time is not independence but interdependence. The elbow room has gone in which a man could 'do what he liked with his own' without denying the same liberty to others. The brute fact of our economic relatedness in 'one world' is borne home upon us ever more pressingly. Neutrality and isolationism are becoming impossible. If we are to survive at all, it is clear that it can be only as 'members one of another'. The line between private and public is blurring. It is the age, for good or for ill, of planning, of welfare service and corporate ownership, and, internationally, of the super-state.

In this situation we are dealing with what Mr. Middleton Murry has called the socialised man. The powers of the individual to act, or even to think, to any significant degree in independence of or against his social milieu are constantly being reduced. It is easy to see this simply as the creeping paralysis of a totalitarian slavery; and, indeed, its conclusion in the frightful prospect of

7

George Orwell's *Nineteen Eighty-Four* is only too depressingly possible. But if, above all, it is the task of Christians to *prevent* such a consummation, we have a duty, before we do anything else, to understand and accept from the hands of God the facts which have produced the socialised man. What these facts are it is no purpose of this essay to diagnose. But we shall be able to offer an alternative to modern slavery that is socially relevant only if it is one that has fully, and positively, taken them into account.

This means, among other things, that our ideal of freedom, and of the free society, cannot be defined simply in terms of *in*dependence. The redemption of man to-day means his release to become, not an individual—for in independence he is powerless in the face of the giant State—but a person, who may find rather than lose himself in the interdependence of the community. The content of social salvation for the modern man is to discover himself as a person, as one who freely chooses interdependence because his nature is to be made for others, rather than as one who is engulfed in it because the pressures of his age demand it. The alternative to the 'They' is not the 'I' but the 'We'.

The second basic conviction from which this book springs is that in the Pauline concept of the body there is something of profound implication and relevance both for the understanding of this problem (which, it must be remembered, is nothing less than *the* social, political and religious problem of our age) and for its Christian solution.

Paul starts, as we do, from the fact that man is bound up in a vast solidarity of historical existence which denies him freedom to control his own destiny or achieve his true end. This is the 'body' of sin and death, in which he is involved at every level of his being, physical, political and even cosmic. The great corporations of modern society are expressions of this all-embracing solidarity. The temptation of Western man is to seek salvation by exalting the individual *against* such collectives or by seeking withdrawal from the body of socio-historical existence. Paul saw that the Christian gospel is very different. For the body is not simply evil: it is made by God and for God. Solidarity is the divinely ordained structure in which personal life is to be lived. Man's freedom does not lie in the fact that he is not bound, nor his individuality in the fact that he is not social. Both derive from an unconditional and inalienable responsibility to God, which is not denied by the solidarities of the body and can indeed be discharged only in and through them. Christians should be the last people to be found clinging to the wrecks of an atomistic individualism, which has no foundation in the Bible. For their hope does not lie in escape from collectivism: it lies in the resurrection of the body—that is to say, in the redemption, transfiguration, and ultimate supersession of one solidarity by another. This is Paul's gospel of the new corporeity of the Body of Christ, which itself depends on the redemptive act wrought by Jesus in the body of His flesh through death.

One could say without exaggeration that the concept of the body forms the keystone of Paul's theology. In its closely inter-connected meanings, the word σῶμα (*soma*) knits together all his great themes. It is from the body of sin and death that we are delivered; it is through the body of Christ on the Cross that we are saved; it is into His body the Church that we are incorporated; it is by His body in the Eucharist that this Community is sustained; it is in our body that its new life has to be manifested; it is to a resurrection of this body to the likeness of His glorious body that we are destined. Here, with the exception of the doctrine of God, are represented all the main tenets of the Christian Faith—the doctrines of Man, Sin, the Incarnation and Atonement, the Church, the Sacraments, Sanctification, and Eschatology. To trace the subtle links and interaction between the different senses of this word σῶμα is to grasp the thread that leads through the maze of Pauline thought.

Nor is this concept of the body the key only to the *unity* of the Apostle's theology; it is also perhaps the most striking mark of its *distinctiveness*. For no other New Testament writer has the word σῶμα any doctrinal significance. The whole development of the *theology* of the body is characteristically his own. And with it is bound up most of his peculiar contribution both to the thought and the discipline of the early Church.

It is therefore remarkable that there exists, as far as I am aware, no study which seeks to correlate all Paul's language on the body. The nearest thing is Prof. Ernst Käsemann's *Leib und Leib Christi* (Tübingen, 1933), to which I am particularly indebted for the Old Testament and Pauline understanding of man. But this omits all discussion of the vitally important redemption of the body through Christ's work on the Cross. Moreover, it is more concerned with the external sources of the author's language than with the doctrinal content of his teaching. Fr. Lionel Thornton, again, in his great work *The Common Life in the Body of Christ* (1941) covers Paul's treatment of the Body of Christ in all its forms, but takes no account of his basic definitions of the body, the flesh, and so on, in his doctrine of man. The large number of other more general books on Pauline theology to which I am under obligation will appear in the body of the text.

For the purpose of this essay I have taken as Pauline all the New Testament epistles written under his name, with the exception of 1 and 2 *Timothy* and *Titus*, and, of course, *Hebrews*. This is not the place to argue questions of authorship. I can only say that I am unconvinced by the reasons for rejecting *Ephesians*. I believe it can be shown that the understanding of σῶμα (which in this epistle above all is the key word) is essentially continuous both here and in *Colossians* with the rest of Paul's usage. On the other hand, the omission of the word altogether from the Pastorals seems as decisive an argument against their Pauline authorship, at any rate in their present form, as any that can be advanced.

All Biblical quotations are from the Revised Version, except where a change has been necessary to bring out the sense of the original.

CHAPTER ONE

THE BODY OF THE FLESH

(1) THE OLD TESTAMENT BACKGROUND

IT is fairly generally conceded to-day that, however much Paul may have drawn on Hellenistic sources for other parts of his doctrine, he is at any rate in his anthropology fundamentally what he describes himself, a Hebrew of the Hebrews. There are indeed individual words[1] and extensions of usage which are to be explained from other sources. But the basic categories with which he works derive from the Old Testament view of man, and presuppose the questions and interests upon which that view rests. This contention should receive full justification in the course of this chapter.

Nevertheless, one is at once confronted by the remarkable fact that for the key word σῶμα (*soma*), body, there is, strictly, no Old Testament background. Or, rather, the Old Testament background consists paradoxically in the important fact that the Hebrews had no term for the 'body'. In the Septuagint the Greek word σῶμα translates no less than eleven Hebrew words (with cognates, thirteen), for none of which is it a true equivalent.[2]

---

[1] *E.g.*, νοῦς, συνείδησις, and ὁ ἔσω ἄνθρωπος.

[2] It would be more accurate to say that Hebrew has no word for 'the body' which is in any sense technical or doctrinally significant. Of the various words for which σῶμα stands in the LXX, the occurrence of some is virtually accidental: *viz.*, *haïl* (Gen. 34.29—corresponding to σώματα for slaves, as in Rev. 18.13), *taph* (Gen. 47.12, 'according to their families'), *nephesh* (Gen. 36.6, 'souls', *i.e.*, persons), *'or* ('skin', Job 19.26). Others refer only to a dead body, just as σῶμα is frequently so used in the New Testament (*e.g.*, Matt. 14.12; 27.52, 58 f; Luke 17.37; Acts 9.40; Jude 9), though not, as it happens, by Paul. These words are *gûphāh* (1 Chron. 10.12), *nᵉbhēlāh* (Deut. 21.23; Joshua 8.29; 1 Kings 13.22, 24, 28 f), *peger* (Gen. 15.11; Isa. 37.36). Five other words remain. Of these, *shᵉ'ēr* is 'flesh', and is translated by σῶμα only in Prov. 5.11; 11.17. In the former instance it is joined with the much commoner *bāsār*. This again means 'flesh' and is represented normally by σάρξ (143 times). Only in twenty-one instances is it rendered by σῶμα. The distribution of these is as follows: Leviticus, fourteen times (eleven in one chapter); Numbers, three; 1 Kings, one; Job, two; Daniel, one. *Gāv* (1 Kings, 14.9; Neh. 9.26; Ezek. 23.35) means 'back', and is translated by σῶμα only in the phrase 'to cast something behind one's back', *i.e.*, behind oneself. *Gēv* (Job 20.25) also means 'back'. The third of these cognate words, *gᵉviah*, is much nearer to 'body' proper. But it is of no theological significance. It is an uncommon word and occurs as σῶμα only in nine instances, in

The most important term that it represents, and the only one of theological significance, is the word *basar*. It is here if anywhere that one must look for the Old Testament determination of the Pauline use of σῶμα. Yet *basar* is essentially not 'body' but 'flesh', and is in fact in the great majority of instances translated in the Septuagint by σάρξ (*sarx*). This means that both the most decisive words in Pauline anthropology, 'flesh' and 'body', represent a common Hebrew original.

Now, if we ask why it was that the Jews here made do with one word (*basar*) where the Greeks required two (σάρξ and σῶμα), we come up against some of the most fundamental assumptions of Hebraic thinking about man. Our contention will be that the Pauline use of σάρξ and σῶμα is to be understood only in the light of these assumptions, and, consequently, that the Greek presuppositions, which necessarily demanded two words instead of one, are simply misleading if made the starting point in interpreting Paul's meaning. When it is remembered that our modern use of the terms 'body' and 'flesh' is almost wholly conditioned by these Hellenic presuppositions, it is clear that great care must .be observed if we are not to read into Paul's thought ideas which are foreign to him.[1]

To this end a preliminary examination of Hebraic assumptions about man is important.

---

four of which it means a 'corpse' (1 Sam. 31.10, 12 (*bis*) and Nahum 3.3). The other occurrences are: Gen. 47.18 and Neh. 9.37 (in the plural to mean 'selves'); Ezek. 1.11, 23 (of the bodies of the living creatures); and Dan. 10.6 (where it is the 'trunk' and is placed alongside the other parts of the body, not over against them as the whole. Finally, there is the word *geshem* which occurs only in Daniel (seven times) and is of Chaldean origin.

In the apocryphal books, where the writers are expressing themselves originally in Greek, σῶμα is still to be understood for the most part as if it were translating these various Hebrew words. Thus, it represents the O.T. *basar* for the physical body (Judith 10.3; Wis. 18.22; Ecclus. 30.14, 15, 16; 2 Macc. 3.17; 7.7, etc.), particularly as an instrument of sex (Ecclus. 23.16; 47.19), and for the whole self (Ecclus. 7.24; 51.2). In 2 Macc. 12.26 it stands, like *nephesh*, for mere numbers of persons. In Tob. 10.10 and 2 Macc. 8.11 it is used for slaves, and frequently for a corpse (Tob. 1 18; Judith 13.9; Ecclus. 38.16; 41.11; 44.14; 48.13; Bel 32; 1 Macc. 11.4; 2 Macc. 9.29; 12.39). In Wisdom and 4 Maccabees (and to some extent also in 2 Maccabees) Greek influence becomes paramount in a distinction and contrast between body and soul, between a man's outer, perishable frame and his inner, immortal self.

[1] A particularly glaring example of this is the way Prof. R. Bultmann, for all his

It is possible to account for the difference in vocabulary we have noted only on the presupposition that the Hebrews never posed, like the Greeks, certain questions, the answer to which would have forced them to differentiate the 'body' from the 'flesh'. These questions can best be formulated by asking what were the notions to which the Greeks opposed the idea of the body and in contrast with which they found themselves defining it.

(i) The first opposition, basic to Greek thought, is that between *form* and *matter*. A body is the concrete result of a certain form imposed upon and giving definition to a certain stuff. The body, therefore, can be contrasted with the matter or substance out of which it is made—*e.g.* wood, or flesh, or flesh and bones, etc. This contrast is never made by the Hebrews. They required therefore no second term to denote the difference: *basar* stands for the whole life-substance of men or beasts as organised in corporeal form.

(ii) Closely connected with this is the typical Greek contrast between the *one* and the *many*, the whole and its parts. A body stood over against its component parts or organs, each of which had its own function. The Hebrew made no such opposition. Consequently, though there are about eighty parts of the body named in the Old Testament, there is no word for the whole. Almost any part can be used to represent the whole, and the powers and functions of the personality are regarded as exercised through a great variety of organs, indifferently physical and psychical.[1]

Biblicism, gives Paul's understanding of σῶμα as 'the self as the object of its own consciousness or action'—the 'me' rather than the 'I' (*Theologie des N.T.*, I, 192). Such a way of thinking is essentially un-Hebraic and indeed post-Cartesian.

The conception of the σῶμα 'as the organised individual self' (C. H. Dodd, *Romans*, 90) (the whole personality, which is made up of σάρξ and ψυχή), which I stated as the Pauline view in my book *In the End, God . . .*, I now see to be foreign to the Hebrew way of thinking about man. σῶμα, σάρξ and ψυχή all represent the whole man under different aspects.

[1] It is significant that Dr. Aubrey Johnson in a very full discussion of the significance of the different parts of the body for the Hebrew doctrine of man (*The Vitality of the Individual in the Life of Ancient Israel*) never once mentions a word for the body itself. He sees the constant representation of the whole by the part as an instance of that 'grasping of a totality' (Pedersen) so characteristic of Hebrew thought and of which he writes: 'It is, perhaps, hardly too much to say that it is the "open

(iii) It follows from this that the third and perhaps most far-reaching of all the Greek antitheses, that between *body* and *soul*, is also foreign to the Hebrew. The Hellenic conception of man has been described as that of an angel in a slot machine, a soul (the invisible, spiritual, essential ego) incarcerated in a frame of matter, from which it trusts eventually to be liberated. The body is non-essential to the personality: it is something which a man possesses, or, rather, is possessed by. 'The Hebrew idea of the personality', on the other hand, wrote the late Dr. Wheeler Robinson in a sentence which has become famous, 'is an animated body, and not an incarnated soul' (*The People and the Book*, 362). Man does not *have* a body, he *is* a body. He is flesh-animated-by-soul, the whole conceived as a psycho-physical unity: 'The body is the soul in its outward form' (J. Pedersen, *Israel*, I-II, 171). There is no suggestion that the soul is the essential personality, or that the soul (*nephesh*) is immortal, while the flesh (*basar*) is mortal. The soul does not survive a man—it simply goes out, draining away with the blood.[1]

sesame" which unlocks the secrets of the Hebrew language and reveals the riches of the Israelite mind' (*ib.*, 7 f). He opposes this view to Wheeler Robinson's theory of a 'diffusion of consciousness', by virtue of which the various organs and limbs of the body are regarded as functioning independently and self-operatively (*ib.*, 83).

On the Old Testament understanding of man as a whole, and for the basis of the generalisations here made, *vide*:

H. Wheeler Robinson, 'Hebrew Psychology in Relation to Pauline Anthropology', 1902, published in *Mansfield College Essays*, 1909; *The Christian Doctrine of Man*, 1911 (Ch. 1); 'Hebrew Psychology', *The People and the Book* (ed. A. S. Peake), 1925; *Inspiration and Revelation in the Old Testament*, 1946 (Ch. 5).

E. D. Burton, *Spirit, Soul and Flesh*, 1918.

J. Pedersen, *Israel*, 1920 (E. T. 1926), I-II, 99-181.

P. Dhorme, *L'emploi métaphorique des noms de parties du corps en hébreu et en accidien*, 1923.

E. Käsemann, *Leib und Leib Christi*, 1933, 1-23.

W. Eichrodt, *Theologie des Alten Testaments*, 1935 (II).

A. R. Johnson, *The One and the Many in the Israelite Conception of God*, 1942; *The Vitality of the Individual in the Thought of Ancient Israel*, 1949.

[1] The soul or life-power is characteristically described as emptied or poured out unto death (Isa. 53.12; *n.b.* the echo of this in Phil. 2.7 f: 'He emptied himself ... unto death'; and *cf*. Ps. 141.8 (R.V.M.) and 2 Sam. 14.14). Consequently, the dead are not souls, as opposed to bodies, but shadows (*rephaim*, the weak; *cf*. Isa. 14.10, where the fallen king of Babylon is welcomed to Sheol with the words: 'Art thou also become weak as we?'). The dead are unsubstantial, but not immaterial; and death is not extinction, but the weakest form of life. *Vide* especially Pedersen, *op. cit.*, I-II, 179-81, and Johnson, *The Vitality of the Individual in the Thought of Ancient Israel*, 89-107.

(iv) The fourth point of contrast comes out in the Greek description of a body in terms of its *boundary* (ὁρισμός), the frontier by which it is defined from the next self or object. Thus σῶμα as opposed to σάρξ is the principle of individuation, that which marks off and isolates one man from another. The Hebrews, by the very fact that they did not require two words at this point, showed that they did not regard this distinction as fundamental. Or, rather, even when the primitive idea of 'corporate personality' began to cede a place to genuine individuality, the locus of individuation was not found at this point. True individuality was seen to be grounded solely in the indivisible responsibility of each man to God (Jer. 31.29 f; Ezek. 18; Deut. 24.16; *cf*. W. Eichrodt, *Man in the Old Testament*, 9, 23 f). It rested, that is to say, in the uniqueness of the Divine word or call to every man, which demanded from him an inalienable response. It did not in any way reside in him as *basar*. The flesh-body was not what partitioned a man off from his neighbour; it was rather what bound him in the bundle of life with all men and nature, so that he could never make his unique answer to God as an isolated individual, apart from his relation to his neighbour. The *basar* continued, even in the age of greater religious individualism, to represent the fact that personality is essentially social. There was therefore no need *at this point* to have a separate word, corresponding to the Greek σῶμα, to mark the contrast with the non-individuating 'flesh'.

The discussion of this last contrast goes some way to indicate the reason why the Hebrews were content to leave unasked so many questions which seemed to the Greeks, as they seem to us, so obvious. It is indeed difficult to think about the body for its own sake without being forced to define it in terms of these contrasts. The answer is quite simply that the Hebrews did not think about the body for its own sake. They were not interested in the body as such. All questions of the interrelation of its different parts and functions were entirely subordinated to the question of the relation of the whole man, as part of the solidarity of creation, to God. All Hebrew thinking was done, as it were, in this vertical dimension of man's relatedness to God as a creature and as a fallen creature. The Hebrew never abstracted man from this relationship and set him up on a pedestal, apart from the rest of creation, to exclaim 'What a piece of work is man!' Rather, viewing him in the context of God's total handiwork, he was led to ask: 'When I consider thy heavens, the work of thy fingers, the moon and the stars, which thou hast ordained, what is man that *thou* art mindful of him? And the son of man, that *thou* visitest him?' (Ps. 8.3 f).

Consequently, all words pertaining to the life and constitution of man are to be seen as designating or qualifying this fundamental relationship of man to God. The parts of the body are thought of, not primarily from the point of view of their difference from, and interrelation with, other parts, but as signifying or stressing different aspects of the whole man in relation to God. From the standpoint of analytic psychology and physiology the usage of the Old Testament is chaotic: it is the nightmare of the anatomist when any part can stand at any moment for the whole and similar functions be predicated of such various organs as the heart, the kidneys and the bowels—not to mention the soul. But such usage is admirably adapted to expressing the unity of the personality under the various aspects of its fundamental relation to God. The Hebrew had little or no interest or competence in psychology or physiology. But that must not blind us to the fact that there is in the Old Testament a profound anthropology or doctrine of man.[1] All the richness of Semitic terminology in respect of the body and its functions was devoted to expressing a deep understanding of the *theological* truth of man's nature.

If these interests and presuppositions are borne in mind they will illuminate much of what Paul is saying and forearm us to some extent against false and anachronistic interpretations of his thought. To his usage we may now move.

---

[1] *cf.* E. Käsemann, *op. cit.*, 23.

(2) THE PAULINE USAGE

Since the purpose of this essay is simply to analyse Paul's understanding of the body, it is unnecessary to go in any detail into his
use of other terms, such as ψυχή (*psyche*), soul, and πνεῦμα (*pneuma*),
spirit, which are of great importance for his doctrine of man in
general. But it is essential to pay close attention, not only to
σῶμα, but also to the other word which translates the same Hebrew
basar, namely σάρξ, which, for Pauline anthropology as well as
for that of the Septuagint, is the more fundamental and much
the more frequent of the two.[1]

(i) *The Concept of the Flesh (σάρξ)*

The basic meaning of σάρξ, as of *basar*, is the flesh-substance
common to men and beasts. Except in 1 Cor. 15.39 ('All flesh
is not the same flesh: but there is one flesh of men, and another
flesh of beasts, and another flesh of birds, and another of fishes'),
Paul confines σάρξ to human flesh. He follows the Septuagint in
preferring κρέας for animal meat (Rom. 14.21; 1 Cor. 8.13).

Though σάρξ means flesh-substance, it is not thought of as the
stuff out of which a σῶμα is formed and as such contrasted with it.[2]
Nor, again, is it to be understood as a *part* of the body (though,
in technical Greek, it is the soft, muscular parts). Rather, it is the
whole body, or, better, the whole person, considered from the

---

[1] This fact in itself indicates how determinative is the Old Testament background
for the Pauline doctrine of man. The current anthropology of hellenised Judaism,
while formally retaining the traditional phrases, preferred to work, not with the
(psychologically crude) category of the 'flesh', but with the antithesis of 'body' and
'soul' (*cf.* E. Käsemann, *op. cit.*, 19-22). As we shall see, these latter terms occur
together only once in the Pauline writings (1 Thess. 5.23) and are never contrasted.

[2] Käsemann (*op. cit.*, 101) and Bultmann (*op. cit.*, I, 229) see 1 Cor. 15.35-49 as an
exception to this typically Old Testament usage. But the contrast in this passage
is not between the body and the different kinds of substance or flesh out of which
it is composed, but between different kinds of bodies, different kinds of flesh,
different kinds of glory. The word 'flesh' (in v. 39) is quite incidental and is perhaps
introduced at all only in order to avoid another repetition of the word 'body',
which already occurs in vv. 37, 38 and 40. The whole verse, and with it every
mention of the σάρξ, could actually be omitted without affecting the sense of the
passage. In v. 44 Paul contrasts the σῶμα πνευματικόν with the σῶμα ψυχικόν (not
σάρκινον, made of flesh); but this is not to be understood in terms of form and
substance, as will become clear in the course of later discussion.

point of view of his external, physical existence. Thus, Gal. 4. 13 f ('Ye know that because of an infirmity of the flesh, I preached the gospel unto you the first time'), 2 Cor. 12.7 ('There was given me a thorn in the flesh') and 1 Cor. 7.28 ('Such (*i.e.*, the married) shall have tribulation in the flesh') refer generally to physical distress without further specification. 'The flesh' is so used for the incarnation of Christ (Eph. 2.15; Col. 1.22) and of a person's bodily presence (Col. 2.1, 5).

It is a natural extension from this for σάρξ to stand for anything external and visible, as opposed to what is internal and spiritual. 'He is not a Jew, which is one outwardly; neither is that circumcision, which is outward in the flesh; but he is a Jew, which is one inwardly; and circumcision is that of the heart, in the spirit, not in the letter' (Rom. 2.28 f; *cf.* Eph. 2.11). The flesh corresponds to 'the outward' (Rom. 2.28), 'the outward man' (2 Cor. 4.16), 'the things which are seen' (2 Cor. 4.18), 'the letter' (Rom. 2.27, 29; 7.6; 2 Cor. 3.6). It is opposed to the inward man, the heart (*cf.* 2 Cor. 5.12, 'they that glory in appearance, and not in heart'), the spirit ('to deliver such a one unto Satan for the destruction of the flesh, that the spirit may be saved', 1 Cor. 5.5).[1]

It is, however, important, against any interpretation derived from isolating the last quotation with its contrast between flesh and spirit, to insist again that σάρξ does not mean one part of a man, but the whole man seen under the aspect of the flesh. Hence it frequently stands, as in the Old Testament, simply for 'man'. 'I conferred not with flesh and blood' (Gal. 1.16) means 'with no other human beings'. 'No flesh', in the regular Old Testament phrase, means 'nobody' (Rom. 3.20; Gal. 2.16; 1 Cor. 1.29. The last instance should be compared with Eph. 2.9, where the phrase μή τις is an exact parallel of μὴ πᾶσα σάρξ). So, very often, the word 'flesh' is interchangeable with the personal pronoun—for

---

[1] The adjective σαρκικός similarly covers anything external and material (not merely 'fleshly'). *Cf.* Rom. 15.27: 'For if the Gentiles have been made partakers of their spiritual things, they owe it to them also to minister unto them in carnal things', and 1 Cor. 9.11: 'If we sowed unto you spiritual things, is it a great matter if we shall reap your carnal things?'

instance, in Eph. 5.28 f: 'He that loveth his own wife loveth himself: for no man ever hated his own flesh.' In 2 Cor. 7.5, 'Our flesh had no relief' is simply a periphrasis for 'I' (it is indistinguishable from 'I had no relief for my spirit' in 2 Cor. 2.13), and the explanatory words 'without were fightings, within were fears' make it clear that the flesh does not here refer simply to the external body. So, in Col. 1.24, to 'fill up . . . that which is lacking of the afflictions of Christ in my flesh' means 'in my person'. Similarly, 'in our mortal flesh' (2 Cor. 4.11) = 'in us as mortal'; 'because of the infirmity of your flesh' (Rom. 6.19) = 'seeing you are weak people'. Finally, in Rom. 7.18, 'in me, that is in my flesh, dwelleth no good thing' is equivalent to saying that for me, *qua* σάρξ, 'to will is present . . . , but to do that which is good is not'.

But it is not without significance that the word 'flesh' should be that used for the person in these instances. For they illustrate well the particular aspect under which man is seen when he is designated σάρξ. Here again Paul faithfully represents the Old Testament usage. Man as *basar*, though defined essentially in his relation to God, 'the God of all flesh' (Jer. 32.27), is yet man in his distance and difference from God. For while God is Spirit, He is not flesh: 'Hast thou eyes of flesh? or seest thou as man seeth?' (Job 10.4); 'the Egyptians are men, and not God; and their horses flesh, and not spirit' (Isa. 31.3). Flesh represents mere man, man in contrast with God—hence man in his weakness and mortality.[1]

So, for Paul, while πνεῦμα, spirit, when it is used of man, is that in virtue of which he is open to and transmits the life of God (Rom. 8.16; *cf.* 1 Cor. 2.10 f), σάρξ is man in contrast with God. In Rom. 2.29, the antithesis 'in the spirit, not in the letter (= the flesh)' stands parallel to 'whose praise is not of men, but of God'. To have 'conferred with flesh and blood' (Gal. 1.16) would have been for the Apostle to lay himself open to the charge that his gospel was merely human, that it was 'after man' and not 'through revelation' (Gal. 1.11 f; *cf.* 1 Cor. 9.8). Wisdom that is 'fleshly'

[1] *Cf.* Gen. 6.3; Isa. 40.6; Ps. 56.4; 78.39; (*cf.* 103.14); Job 34.15; Jer. 17.5.

(2 Cor. 1.12) or 'after the flesh' (1 Cor. 1.26) is simply 'the wisdom of men' (1 Cor. 2.5, 13).

Such wisdom is at once opposed to 'the power of God' (1 Cor. 2.5), and this indicates one of the two constant characteristics of man as σάρξ. Contrasted with God, who is essentially Spirit, Power (*ruach*, δύναμις), man is impotent. 'Infirmity' is an inherent quality of the σάρξ (Gal. 4.13; Rom. 6.19; *cf.* Rom. 8.3). To act 'according to the flesh' is to do so simply in the fallible power of human strength and resolution: 'When I was thus minded, did I show fickleness? or the things that I purpose, do I purpose according to the flesh, that with me there should be the yea yea and the nay nay?' (2 Cor. 1.17). In the same way, it is weakness (not sensuality) of which Paul is accused by some when they 'count of us as if we walked according to the flesh' (2 Cor. 10.2). This is clear from his reply: 'We do not war according to the flesh (for the weapons of our warfare are not of the flesh, but mighty before God to the casting down of strong holds)' (2 Cor. 10.3 f). The same idea underlies Eph. 6.10-12: 'Be strong in the Lord . . . for our wrestling is not against flesh and blood, but against . . . spiritual hosts.' The contrast is not, as it is commonly taken, between the visible and invisible, but between the ineffectiveness of merely human forces and the 'powers' of the spirit-world. Similarly, in 1 Cor. 15.43 f, the natural (*i.e.*, fleshly) body is sown in 'weakness', the spiritual body is raised in 'power'.[1]

The second abiding characteristic of man as σάρξ, in his distance from God, is his mortality. In distinction from the quickening power of the living God, flesh is 'mortal' (2 Cor. 4.11; *cf.* 'this mortal' of 1 Cor. 15.53 f). The outer man 'is decaying day by day' (2 Cor. 4.16); 'the things that are seen' are πρόσκαιρα (2 Cor. 4.18), not, that is, temporal as opposed to timeless, but temporary. Similarly, what can be handled, tasted and touched is all to 'perish with the using' (Col. 2.21f; *cf.* 1 Cor. 6.13). 'Flesh and blood

---

[1] Paul is again faithful to the Old Testament (*vide* Pedersen, *op. cit.*, I-II, 176) in placing the contrast between the weakness of σάρξ and the strength of πνεῦμα not within man but between man and the superhuman (particularly God). Contrast Mark 14.38: 'The spirit indeed is willing, but the flesh is weak.'

cannot inherit the kingdom of God' for the reason that 'corruption doth not inherit incorruption' (1 Cor. 15.50). It is this perishable nature of the σάρξ which provides the possibility of death being imposed on man as punishment (see below p. 34). The flesh can be delivered for destruction (1 Cor. 5.5); and 'he that soweth unto his own flesh' (*i.e.*, lives simply as σάρξ) 'shall of the flesh reap corruption' (Gal. 6.8).

Now, man as 'flesh' is related to God in this way, not as an individual, but as part of the whole world-order. Here again the typical Old Testament presuppositions come to the surface in Pauline thought. For man over against God is man as a creature, bound up in the bundle of created existence. Hence σάρξ for Paul means man in his 'worldliness', in the solidarity of earthly existence. To 'abide in the flesh' (Phil. 1.24) is to continue living in this life (*cf.* Gal. 2.20: 'the life that I now live in the flesh'). In Philem. 16, 'a brother . . . both in the flesh and in the Lord' means, as Moffatt translates, 'as a man and as a Christian'. So in Col. 3.22 and Eph. 6.5 he speaks of 'your masters according to the flesh', *i.e.*, in this world.

In this connection, σάρξ, again like *basar* in the Old Testament, stands especially for the solidarities of sex ('the twain shall become one flesh', 1 Cor. 6.16; Eph. 5.31) and of race ('my kinsmen according to the flesh', Rom. 9.3, contracted to 'my flesh' in Rom. 11.14). So, in Rom. 4.1, Paul speaks of 'Abraham, our forefather according to the flesh', and says of Christ that He was 'born of the seed of David according to the flesh' (Rom. 1.3) and was an Israelite τὸ κατὰ σάρκα, in what concerned race (Rom. 9.5).

This usage constantly tends to fall over into a contrast (already implicit in the τό of Rom. 9.5) between mere external, racial connection and what is of real, spiritual, divine import. 'Israel after the flesh' (1 Cor. 10.18) is distinguished from the Christian Church, the true Israel of God. In Gal. 4.23 and 29, the son born 'after the flesh' is contrasted with the one born 'through promise' and 'after the Spirit'. In Rom. 8.9, the antithesis becomes quite stark: 'It is not the children of the flesh that are children of God.'

This prepares the way for a vital transition in the Pauline understanding of σάρξ. For, man as σάρξ, as part of the world, stands always in a relation of ambiguity to God, since the world to which he is bound in the flesh is a world fallen under sin and death. The order that at present obtains is controlled by powers organised in opposition to God—the rulers (1 Cor. 2.6, 8), the god (2 Cor. 4.4), the spirit (1 Cor. 2.12), the elements (Gal. 4.3; Col. 2.8, 20), of this age.[1] Consequently, to be 'in the flesh'[2] is to be subject to the powers that control it. In Rom. 7.6, 'that wherein we were holden' refers to the σάρξ: it is that by virtue of which the powers have their grip over us. (The σάρξ is personified as a force rather than as a sphere in the phrase κατὰ σάρκα, and in Rom. 8.12; 13.14; Gal. 5.13.)

Because man as σάρξ is thus involved in an order of creation which is, at one and the same time, of God's willing and yet in antagonism to Him, there is an inherent tension and contradiction in all phrases relating to man's life in this world. On the one hand, to be 'in the flesh' is man's natural and God-given form of earthly existence (Gal. 2.20, etc.). Christians cannot 'go out of the world' (1 Cor. 5.10) while they live this life. And whether they 'abide in the flesh' (Phil. 1.24) or not, whether 'at home or absent', they 'make it their aim . . . to be well-pleasing' to the Lord (2 Cor. 5.9). And yet, for Paul, to be ἐν σαρκί stands also for

[1] It is probable that in the unique combination of Eph. 2.2 (κατὰ τὸν αἰῶνα τοῦ κόσμου τούτου), ὁ αἰών should be seen as a similar personification, and the phrase rendered 'in obedience to the aeon, or controlling spirit, of this world'. It would then stand in exact apposition to the following phrase: κατὰ τὸν ἄρχοντα τῆς ἐξουσίας τοῦ ἀέρος, according to the ruler of the power of the air. There is, of course, abundant parallel for such personification in contemporary Gnostic thought. This interpretation is adopted by W. L. Knox, *St. Paul and the Church of the Gentiles*, 187.

[2] Käsemann (*op. cit.*, 103) points out that this phrase ἐν σαρκί, as well as κατὰ σάρκα, is a remarkable one. Neither is to be paralleled in Hellenistic thought, where flesh is simply a part of the body, and the Greek idea of the soul being in (the tomb of) the body is not what Paul is meaning. The usage is equally strange to the Old Testament, where man *is* flesh rather than *in* the flesh. Paul's thought at this point may well be influenced by the Gnostic idea of a semi-personified sphere of being (αἰών) outside man, to whose powers an individual is subject as long as he remains in it. 'In the flesh' means within the sphere, and therefore the jurisdiction, of the world and its forces. It is to be understood in the light of the parallel phrases, 'in Christ' and 'in the Spirit'.

something incompatible with being a Christian. It is a sphere in which Christians no longer are (*cf.* Rom. 7.5: 'when we were in the flesh' and Rom. 8.9: 'but ye are not in the flesh'); for '*they that are in the flesh cannot please God*' (Rom. 8.8), 'because the mind of the flesh is enmity against God' (Rom. 8.7).

This ambiguity is particularly apparent in the phrase κατὰ σάρκα. As we have seen, it is used to designate the purely natural, God-ordained ties of genealogy. Israelites according to the flesh are those who are 'by nature Jews' (Gal. 2.15).[1] And yet the purely natural man[2] cannot receive the things of the Spirit of God (1 Cor. 2.14). To know any man, or to know Christ, 'after the flesh' is to miss the whole truth of what God has wrought in His new act of creation (2 Cor. 5.16 f—κατὰ σάρκα should be taken here with the verb and not as referring to the days of Christ's 'flesh'). In 2 Cor. 10.3, κατὰ σάρκα is contrasted with ἐν σαρκί as describing what is unchristian as opposed to what is natural and God-given: 'Though we walk in the flesh, we do not war according to the flesh.' In Rom. 8.4-7, Christians are those who walk 'not after the flesh, but after the spirit'. The state of opposition to God and Christ can be described simply as κατὰ σάρκα εἶναι (Rom. 8.5), for those who are such 'mind the things of the flesh': their whole outlook is identified with it and the powers that rule it. To walk κατὰ σάρκα is to walk κατὰ τὸν αἰῶνα τοῦ κόσμου τούτου, according to the

---

[1] φύσις stands under the same moral ambiguity. It is a divinely appointed norm: 'The Gentiles . . . do by nature the things of the law' (Rom. 2.14); 'Doth not even nature itself teach you?' (1 Cor. 11.14; *cf.* Rom. 1.26 f). And yet: 'We also once lived in the lusts of the flesh, doing the desires of the flesh and of the mind, and were by nature children of wrath' (Eph. 2.3).

[2] ψυχικός. This word is virtually interchangeable for Paul with σαρκικός (*cf.* the contrast ψυχικός—πνευματικός in 1 Cor. 2.14 f and πνευματικός—σάρκινος, σαρκικός immediately afterwards in 1 Cor. 3.1, 3). This usage derives from the Old Testament assimilation of *basar* and *nephesh*, σάρξ and ψυχή, to describe the animated body (*cf.* Ps. 63.1: 'my soul thirsteth for thee, my flesh longeth for thee'), and stands in strong contrast with the Greek antithesis between soul and body. In 1 Cor. 15.44-9 ψυχικός is the purely natural, contrasted with πνευματικός and identified with χοϊκός (earthy). (Both the contrast and, still more, the identification would have been an absurdity to the Greeks.) Yet the purely natural, because of the Fall, is unnatural (1 Cor. 2.14). This pejorative use of ψυχικός is even more strongly represented in its only non-Pauline occurrences in the New Testament: 'This wisdom is not a wisdom that cometh down from above, but is earthly, *sensual*, devilish' (James 3.15), and 'These are they who make separations, *sensual*, not having the Spirit' (Jude 19).

aeon of this world (Eph. 2.2 f). It is opposed to living κατὰ πνεῦμα (Rom. 8.4 f), κατὰ κύριον (2 Cor. 11.17), κατὰ ἀγάπην (Rom. 14.15).

It is important to understand exactly what this living 'after the flesh' means and why the 'carnal' can thus stand for what is sinful (*e.g.*, Rom. 7.14).[1]

It cannot be overemphasised that this is not because, as in Greek thinking, matter or the material part of man is inherently and irremediably evil, in contrast with the soul or spirit.[2] When Paul says that 'the flesh lusteth against the Spirit, and the Spirit against the flesh' (Gal. 5.17), he is not referring to the conflict, familiar to Greek ethics, between man's reason and his passions.[3] This should be obvious from the fact that, of 'the works of the flesh' that follow, ten out of fifteen have nothing to do with the sins of sensuality (Gal. 5.19-21). It is further borne out by 1 Cor. 3.3: 'Whereas there is among you jealousy and strife' (*par excellence* 'sins of the spirit'), 'are ye not σαρκικοί, and walk after the manner of men?'.[4]

This final phrase 'and walk after the manner of men' points to the essential wrongness of living κατὰ σάρκα. It is the epitome of

---

[1] This extension of the Old Testament use of flesh to denote moral weakness was not made by Rabbinic Judaism. For all his interest in the Rabbinic background of Paul's thought Mr. W. D. Davies admits, 'the evidence . . . is conclusive that the Rabbis did not develop the ethical connotation that *basar* had in the Old Testament. There are no expressions in Rabbinic Judaism which literally correspond to the use of σάρκινος and σαρκικός and πνευματικός and ψυχικός in Paul.' (*Paul and Rabbinic Judaism*, 20).

[2] On this assumption the exhortation to 'cleanse ourselves from all defilement of flesh and spirit' (2 Cor. 7.1) could not be understood.

[3] Moffatt's translation brings out well how the ἐπιθυμία is on both sides: 'The passion of the flesh is against the passion of the Spirit, and the passion of the Spirit against the flesh.'

[4] There is an interesting progression of ideas in 1 Cor. 3.1-3, which is unfortunately concealed in the English versions by the use of 'carnal' to cover two words. 'Previously', the Apostle is saying to his converts, 'I was not able to talk to you as to "spiritual" (as you would now like); but I had to address you as σάρκινοι (literally, "made of flesh"; *cf.* 2 Cor. 3.3), that is, as immature Christians—people one must treat like babies, as though they were flesh and nothing else. I fed you on slops, not on meat; for you were not at that time capable of anything else. But this time the trouble is different. You are still not capable of being treated as "spiritual" (as Christians should be: 1 Cor. 2.15; Gal. 6.1). But now it is because you are σαρκικοί—yourselves acting as though you were flesh and nothing else. For seeing there is jealousy and schism among you, does not that prove that you are simply flesh-minded, merely unregenerate human nature, with nothing of the divine about you?'

sin, not because the flesh is evil or impure, but because such an attitude is a denial of the human situation over against God. It is not primarily a disturbance of the relation of different parts of man to each other (though that follows: Rom. 1.24 ff), but a distortion of the fundamental relationship of the creature to God. One could describe the situation by saying that σάρξ as neutral is man living in the world, σάρξ as sinful is man living for the world: he becomes 'a man of the world' by allowing his being-in-the-world, itself God-given, to govern his whole life and conduct. To live κατὰ σάρκα is to make 'the belly' one's God and only care (Rom. 16.18; Phil. 3.19).[1] It is to be 'careful for the things of the world' rather than 'for the things of the Lord' (1 Cor. 7.32 f) and its consequence is 'lust' (Gal. 5.16, 24; Rom. 13.14; Eph. 2.3), 'indulgence' (Col. 2.23), 'covetousness' (Col. 3.5). This setting of the mind on the things that are upon earth (Col. 3.2; Phil. 3.19) is essentially idolatry (Col. 3.5). Consequently, as Bultmann rightly stresses (*op. cit.*, I, 235 ff), 'the mind of the flesh' stands primarily for a denial of man's dependence on God and for a trust in what is of human effort or origin. Thus, when Paul asks the Galatians, 'having begun in the Spirit, are ye now perfected in the flesh?' (Gal. 3.3), he refers, not to a lapse into sensuality, but to a return to reliance upon the law. The flesh is concerned with serving 'the letter' (Rom. 7.6; 2.28 f), which is 'of men' (Rom. 2.29) and represents human self-sufficiency (2 Cor. 3.5 f). 'Fleshly wisdom' (2 Cor. 1.12) is a man's trust in his own knowledge and experience, 'taking his stand upon the things which he hath seen, vainly puffed up by his fleshly mind'[2] (Col. 2.18, R.V.M.;

---

[1] Again, this does not refer simply to the sin of gluttony. κοιλία, like the rest of the organs, does not merely describe a *part* of the body; nor does it stand for something sensual. Those who 'serve their own belly' are those who 'cause divisions and occasions of stumbling' (Rom. 16.17 f).

[2] τοῦ νοὸς τῆς σαρκός—another impossible combination for the Greek mind. Though the actual word νοῦς may be taken from Hellenistic terminology, we have here a good example of how, like every other term, it is drawn by Paul into his typically Hebraic usage. It characterises, not a part of a man which is physically exclusive of another part (*e.g.*, the σάρξ), but one aspect of man's total relationship to God (namely, his capacity to recognise and respond to the divine claim upon his life: Rom. 7.22-25; 12.2), which may like everything else be prostituted and subordinated to the attitude that sets man in God's place (*viz.*, living κατὰ σάρκα).

cf. 1 Cor. 8.1). This puffing up results in having confidence in, and glorying after, the flesh, *i.e.*, human righteousness and pedigree (Phil. 3.3 f; Gal. 6.13; 2 Cor. 11.18). This again is equivalent to 'glorying in men' (1 Cor. 3.21), and to 'trusting in ourselves' rather than in 'God who raiseth the dead' (2 Cor. 1.9)[1]: it is 'commending ourselves' and 'glorying in appearance' (2 Cor. 5.12), which is the opposite of 'glorying in the Lord' (1 Cor. 1.31; 2 Cor. 10.17; *cf.* Gal. 6.14). As such it is the final denial of the human situation (1 Cor. 4.7) and must be utterly shattered, 'that no flesh should glory before God' (1 Cor. 1.29).

This is Paul's last word on the σάρξ, and, like his first, it simply recapitulates the message of the Old Testament: 'Cursed is the man that trusteth in man, and maketh flesh his arm, and whose heart departeth from the Lord' (Jer. 17.5).

(ii) *The Concept of the Body* (σῶμα)

While the concept of σάρξ is the key to Paul's anthropology, it is unable to provide the foundation for the remainder of his theology. When it has established man in his 'otherness' from God, in his frailty and mortality, it has nothing more it can do. σῶμα, on the other hand, while it can be identified with σάρξ in all man's sin and corruption, is also the carrier of his resurrection. It is therefore the link between Paul's doctrine of man and his whole gospel of Christ, the Church and eternal life.

The σῶμα, however, can be raised only if it first die. It is, therefore, essential to begin by consolidating the identity between σάρξ and σῶμα, to see how man as σῶμα goes right down to the depth of man as σάρξ, and shares all its distance and death. σῶμα (grounded as it is in the same Hebrew concept of the *basar*) repeats all the emphases of σάρξ before it diverges from it.

---

[1] *Cf.* 2 Cor. 10.7, where 'trusting in oneself' is connected with 'looking at the things that are before one's face', *i.e.*, regarding matters from the point of view of the σάρξ.

In the first place, like σάρξ, σῶμα is the external man,[1] 'the body' as commonly understood. This is its meaning, for instance, in Gal. 6.17 ('I bear branded on my body the marks of Jesus'), 1 Cor. 9.27 ('I buffet my body and bring it into bondage') and 1 Cor. 13.3 ('If I give my body to be burned . . .'). In Col. 2.23 ('which things have indeed a show of wisdom in will-worship, and humility, and severity to the body; but are not of any value against the indulgence of the flesh') there is an interesting contrast between σῶμα in this purely neutral sense and σάρξ as meaning man in rebellion against God; but there is no reason (apart from the obvious literary one) why σάρξ should not here take the place of σῶμα as well.

In this connection, reference should be made to the conjunction of σῶμα, ψυχή and πνεῦμα in 1 Thess. 5.23, and of σῶμα and πνεῦμα in 1 Cor. 7.34. But there is no attempt, any more than in the Old Testament, to regard man as a trichotomy or dichotomy of exclusive elements.[2] Quite apart from the question of presuppositions, the Pauline usage itself is much too fluid. For instance, besides the above, we find the division σάρξ and πνεῦμα in 2 Cor. 7.1, a parallelism between πνεῦμα and ψυχή in Phil. 1.27, and a synonymous use of πνεῦμα and σάρξ by comparing 2 Cor. 2.13 and 2 Cor. 7.5.

σῶμα, like σάρξ, is used to indicate the external presence of the whole man: 'His letters they say are weighty and strong; but his bodily presence is weak' (2 Cor. 10.10). 1 Cor. 5.3 ('I verily, being absent in body but present in spirit')[3] = Col. 2.5 ('Though

[1] As in the case of σάρξ, Paul uses σῶμα only once of a non-human body. In Col. 2.17, it is the solid substance of an object, the thing itself, as opposed to the shadow that it casts before it. It is tempting to see in his phrase here, τὸ δὲ σῶμα τοῦ Χριστοῦ, a reference to the Church (with Augustine, and also Käsemann, *op. cit.*, 142, and Austin Farrer, *The Parish Communion*, ed. A. G. Hebert, 80f); but it must be resisted.

[2] On 1 Thess. 5.23, Wheeler Robinson comments: 'The enumeration is not systematic, but hortatory, to emphasise the completeness of the preservation; it should be compared with the somewhat similar enumeration of Deut. 6.5: "Thou shalt love the Lord thy God with all thy heart, and with all thy soul, and with all thy might" (*Mansfield College Essays*, 280).

[3] The context here indicates that παρὼν τῷ πνεύματι means for Paul something much stronger than the modern English phrase suggests; namely, 'present in the Holy Spirit', in whose δύναμις every Christian, despite geographical distance, is ὡς παρὼν in the συναγωγή of the faithful.

I am absent in the flesh, yet am I with you in spirit') = 1 Thess.
2.17 ('being bereaved of you for a short season in presence
(προσώπῳ) but not in heart').

In Rom. 4.19 ('he [Abraham] considered his own body now as
good as dead'), σῶμα is used, like σάρξ, as the source and carrier
of sexual power.[1] The same understanding underlies 1 Cor. 7.4
('The wife hath not power over her own body, but the husband:
and likewise also the husband hath not power over his own body,
but the wife') and Rom. 1.24 ('that their bodies should be dis-
honoured among themselves'—the meaning of which is explained
in vv. 26 f). Similarly, Paul argues in 1 Cor. 6.13-20, that 'the
body is not for fornication', insisting that 'he that is joined to a
harlot is one body; for, The twain, saith he, shall become one
flesh' (*i.e.*, a single sexual unit).

But this same passage shows how σῶμα, again like σάρξ, does
not mean simply something external to a man himself, something
he *has*. It is what he *is*. Indeed, σῶμα is the nearest equivalent to
our word 'personality'. He that is joined to a harlot does much
more than contract a superficial union with her. Something is
done that reaches down to the very core of the man's being.
Therefore, 'Flee fornication. Every sin that a man doeth is
without the body; but he that committeth fornication sinneth
against his own body' (1 Cor. 6.18).[2] The σῶμα is the whole
person: 'Your body is a temple of the Holy Ghost. . . . Glorify
God therefore in your body' (1 Cor. 6.19 f). The same immediate
transition from the body as the carrier of sex to the body as a
man's very self occurs in Eph. 5.28 f: 'Even so ought husbands
also to love their own wives as their own bodies. He that loveth
his own wife loveth himself: for no man ever hated his own flesh.'
So, in Rom. 12.1, 'present your bodies a living sacrifice' means
'offer yourselves'; and the words of Phil. 1.20, 'Christ shall be

---

[1] This goes back to the Old Testament use of *basar* for the male organ: Gen.
17.13; Lev. 15.2 ff; Ezek. 16.26; 23.20. Hence, of course, the association of the
flesh with circumcision (Gal. 6.12 f; Rom. 2.28; Eph. 2.11; Col. 2.11, 13) and with
genealogy.
[2] *Cf.* Prov. 6.32: 'He that committeth adultery with a woman is void of understanding: He doeth it that would destroy his own soul.'

magnified in my body, whether by life, or by death', refer to the whole personality of the Apostle.

Frequently again, as in the case of σάρξ, σῶμα is simply a periphrasis for the personal pronoun. Consider, for instance, Rom. 6.12 f: 'Let not sin therefore reign in your mortal *body*, that ye should obey the lusts thereof: neither present your *members* unto sin as instruments of unrighteousness; but present *yourselves* unto God'; or 2 Cor. 4.10-12: 'Always bearing about in the *body* the dying of Jesus, that the life also of Jesus may be manifested in our *body*. For we which live are alway delivered unto death for Jesus' sake, that the life also of Jesus may be manifested in our mortal *flesh*. So then death worketh in *us* . . . .' 1 Cor. 6.15 ('*your bodies* are members of Christ') is paralleled by 1 Cor. 12.27 ('*ye* are the body of Christ, and severally members thereof').

Then, once more like σάρξ, σῶμα stands for man as a being 'in the world'. So, of himself, 'caught up even to the third heaven', Paul can write: 'whether in the body, I know not; or whether out of the body, I know not . . .' (2 Cor. 12.2 f). In 2 Cor. 5.10, 'the things done in (through) the body' refer to the actions of a man's earthly life. 'At home in the body' (2 Cor. 5.6) means 'in the solidarities and securities of earthly existence'; while to be 'absent from the body' (2 Cor. 5.8) is a state of 'nakedness' (2 Cor. 5.3). This is because the body for the Hebrew, like the flesh, is what ties men up with each other, rather than what separates them as individuals. The characteristic emphasis comes out very plainly in a sentence in the Epistle to the Hebrews: 'Remember them that are in bonds, as bound with them; them that are evil entreated, as being yourselves also in the body' (Heb. 13.3). The body is that which joins all people, irrespective of individual differences, in life's bundle together. Paul can use the plural σώματα as a substitute for the reflexive pronoun (Rom. 1.24; 8.11; 12.1; 1 Cor. 6.15; Eph. 5.28), but never does he do it to stress individuation. Moreover, he sometimes employs a collective singular where we should expect a plural: *e.g.*, 'waiting for our adoption, to wit the redemption of our body' (Rom. 8.23); or when he speaks of

Jesus Christ fashioning anew 'the body of our humiliation' (Phil. 3.21). The reference is to the whole mass of fallen human nature in which we share as men.[1]

Now, this being in the body not only binds us to the rest of creation; it also, as in the case of the σάρξ, binds us to the powers which control the body. In creation under the Fall these are the powers of sin and death. As a Christian, Paul can look back on this state and say: 'Our old man was crucified with him, that the body of sin might be done away, that we should no longer be in bondage to sin' (Rom. 6.6); again: 'Let not sin reign in your mortal body, that ye should obey the lusts thereof.... Know ye not, that to whom ye present yourselves as servants unto obedience, his servants ye are?' (Rom. 6.12, 16). So there is a σῶμα τῆς ἁμαρτίας (Rom. 6.6), a body that belongs to sin, just as there is a σάρξ ἁμαρτίας (Rom. 8.3). This is the body of 'death' (Rom. 7.24), of 'humiliation' (Phil. 3.21), of 'dishonour' (1 Cor. 15.43). Like the σάρξ, the σῶμα is 'mortal' (Rom. 6.12; 8.11); like the σάρξ, it has its 'lusts' (Rom. 6.12). 'The deeds of the body' in Rom. 8.13 are none other than the results of living κατὰ σάρκα—in fact in some mss. it has become 'the deeds of the flesh'. In Rom. 8.10, 'the body' that 'is dead because of sin' is but a periphrasis for 'the flesh'; while in Rom. 7.22-25, we have the following equivalents: My members (*i.e.*, my σῶμα) = that which is in captivity under the law of sin = the flesh = the opposite of the νοῦς or inner man wherein I delight in the law of God. Col. 3.5 makes the identity of σῶμα with sin even more complete: 'Mortify therefore your members which are upon the earth; fornication, uncleanness, passion, evil desire, and covetousness....' It is here not merely, as in Romans, 'sin in your members': 'your members' are themselves sin.

The identification of σῶμα with σάρξ seems complete. In fact,

---

[1] Too much stress should not be placed upon this as Paul's usage is not consistent, and a comparison, *e.g.*, with his use of καρδία will show a similar alternation between the plural and collective singular. This may be (as in English) a purely grammatical variation; but it may also derive from the 'collective' nature of Hebrew thinking to which Pedersen draws attention in the case of *nephesh* in the Old Testament: 'The word *nephesh* rarely occurs in the plural, because souls which are together are generally taken as a unit' (*op. cit.*, I-II, 165 f). He instances 'our soul' in Num. 11.6; 21.5; Ps. 33.20; 44.25, and 'your soul' in Gen. 23.8 (E.T. 'mind'); Deut. 11.18.

in Col. 2.11, it is closed in the phrase τὸ σῶμα τῆς σαρκός, 'the body of the flesh'—the whole personality organised for, and geared into, rebellion against God. Nevertheless, the very phrase indicates the possibility of a σῶμα which is not τῆς σαρκός.

The identification appears complete, yet careful study reveals that there are significant points at which it is not. The body may in all respects be *identified* with the flesh of sin and death, but the two are not in all respects *identical*. There is no suggestion, for instance, that σῶμα, like σάρξ, in itself connotes weakness and mortality; nor that it carries the imputation of the *merely* external as opposed to the spiritual, the *merely* human as opposed to the divine—so that Paul could speak equally of living κατὰ σῶμα to indicate man setting himself up in the strength of his own creatureliness.

These differences point to the fact that, however much the two may come, through the Fall, to describe the same thing, in essence σάρξ and σῶμα designate different aspects of the human relationship to God. *While σάρξ stands for man, in the solidarity of creation, in his distance from God, σῶμα stands for man, in the solidarity of creation, as made for God.*

This basic contrast comes out most clearly in an important passage already discussed, namely, 1 Cor. 6.13-20: 'Meats for the belly, and the belly for meats: but God shall bring to nought both it and them. But the body is not for fornication, but for the Lord.' The significance of the κοιλία (belly), as we have seen, is the same as that of the σάρξ—something inherently perishable and transient. But the body (which stands throughout this passage for the 'personality') is not created to a purely corruptible function and destiny. One cannot say that all σῶμα is grass: that dust it is and to dust it shall return. Rather, it is 'for the Lord'. While Paul promises no resurrection of the flesh, he proclaims it for the body; whereas man as σάρξ cannot inherit the kingdom of God (1 Cor. 15.50), man as σῶμα can.[1]

---

[1] It is perhaps necessary to insist again that there is no suggestion that σάρξ and σῶμα represent different *parts* of a man's make-up, and that one is mortal and the other not. Each stands for the whole man differently regarded—man as wholly

But he can do so only if he is radically 'changed' (1 Cor. 15.51). The body of sin and humiliation must be 'done away' (Rom. 6.6), 'redeemed' (Rom. 8.23), 'fashioned anew' (Phil. 3.21). The 'natural body' must be transformed to become a 'spiritual body' (1 Cor. 15.44). The natural man cannot know God (1 Cor. 2.14), however much he may have been created to do so (Rom. 1.19 f). 'The body,' indeed, 'is for the Lord.' But Paul is well aware that it is not sufficient simply to repeat that—for the body of human life now belongs securely to the σάρξ and the powers of sin. And in fact he does not repeat it: he rests none of his ethic of the body upon its original creation for God. He knows that such an ethic is futile unless it is grounded in something further. This other truth is not simply that 'the body is for the Lord', but the incredible fact of the Christian gospel that 'the Lord is for the body', and that 'God hath both raised the Lord, and will raise up us through his power' (1 Cor. 6.13 f).[1] αὐτὸς ἐγώ, 'left to myself',[2] says Paul,

perishable, man as wholly destined for God. Prof. P. Althaus' comment is worth quoting: 'The body is, on the one hand, wholly κοιλία, that is, the sum of the sensual functions which make our earthly life possible; as such it passes away with this earthly world. On the other hand, the body is wholly σῶμα, that is, the carrier and object of our action, expression and form; as such it is a limb of the body of the risen Christ and will be raised with the personality' (though the Hebrew would make no such distinction between the body and the personality). 'Because the one and the same body is *both κοιλία and σῶμα,* any concrete or objective expression of what dies, and what is preserved and purified through resurrection is impossible' (*Die letzten Dinge,* 4te Aufl., 130).

It is equally important not to get the relation between σάρξ and σῶμα confused by discussing it in terms of the modern and un-Hebraic category of 'matter'. Neither of them is to be defined in terms of the stuff of which it is composed. σάρξ is indeed the equivalent of matter in the sense of *mere* matter, matter and nothing else ('materialism' is fairly near to living κατὰ σάρκα); but it is certainly not 'matter' as opposed to 'mind'. The higher psychical functions are equally σάρξ, and living for the things of the mind alone would be to live κατὰ σάρκα just as much as pure sensualism (*cf., e.g.,* Paul's condemnation, under this head, of life under the law). σῶμα is also matter as it is created *for* God, but it is not in the least constituted what it is by its being physical. It fulfils its essence by being utterly subject to Spirit, not by being either material or immaterial. Its substance depends entirely on the nature of the medium through which the Spirit is manifesting itself. It is therefore of no theological importance whether Christ in the body of His resurrection appearances could or could not, for instance, eat fish. Again, creation transfigured at the *Parousia* may or may not be physical—its substance is quite irrelevant. All that is certain is that it is as σῶμα and not as σάρξ that it will 'inherit the kingdom of God'.

[1] It is indeed only in the light of the Resurrection and of the glorious destiny of the body revealed in Christ, the firstfruits, that Paul, the Hebrew, comes to see a distinction between σάρξ and σῶμα as essential. The Old Testament, as we have seen, found no need for such distinction.

[2] So L. S. Thornton, *The Common Life in the Body of Christ,* 152.

I am divided and powerless: 'With the mind I serve the law of God; but with the flesh the law of sin' (Rom. 7.25). But now, he writes to his friends, οὐκ ἐστὲ ἑαυτῶν, 'you do not belong to yourselves; for you were bought with a price: glorify God *therefore* in your body' (1 Cor. 6.19 f).

How this redemption and resurrection of the body is made possible is the central theme of Paul's doctrine of the person and work of Christ.

CHAPTER TWO

THE BODY OF THE CROSS

'So we also, when we were children, were held in bondage under the rudiments of the world, but when the fulness of time came, God sent forth his Son, born of a woman, born under the law, that we might receive the adoption of sons' (Gal. 4.3-5). Thus Paul states the full import of his enigmatic phrase in 1 Cor. 6.13: ὁ κύριος τῷ σώματι, 'the Lord for the body'. Into the body of the old world of sin and death enters the Prince of Life, Himself in a body of flesh, to redeem, quicken and transfigure it.

To understand the manner in which Paul sees this accomplished, it is necessary to describe in more detail his picture of the condition of man and its causes which the Incarnation came to reverse.

(1) The human situation is, in the first place, one of *death*. Now, death for the Hebrew is never a purely natural phenomenon. Man as σάρξ is 'of the earth' (1 Cor. 15.48): 'Dust thou art,' says God to Adam (Gen. 3.19). But man, unlike the grass of the field and the beasts, is not merely σάρξ. For all his being as flesh, he is created to live in a unique relationship to his Creator. He is made in the image of God; he is intended, not simply for annihilation, but 'for the Lord'. Consequently, the ensuing phrase of Gen. 3.19, 'and unto dust shalt thou return', is a word of judgment, subsequent upon the Fall. For animals to die is natural; for man to die is unnatural. It is a punishment for sin (Rom. 1.32, etc.); and it is no arbitrary punishment, being bound up with it by an inner necessity. For to live 'after the flesh', on the assumption, namely, that man's life consists simply in the σάρξ, in his self-sufficiency apart from God, is *ipso facto* to accept the end of the σάρξ as the end of man, that is, dissolution and death. 'If ye live after the flesh ye must die' (Rom. 8.13); 'he that soweth to his own flesh, shall of the flesh reap corruption' (Gal. 6.8). The fruit, the wages, the consummation (Rom. 6.21, 23; 7.5) of life κατὰ σάρκα is quite inevitably death. Indeed, 'the mind of the

34

flesh *is* death' (Rom. 8.6). It is for this reason too that the old covenant is a διακονία τοῦ θανάτου, an administration which issues in death, and its glory καταργουμένη, hasting to destruction (2 Cor. 3.6-11). For it is a dispensation of 'the letter' which 'killeth', and 'the letter', as we have seen, stands for the righteousness of the flesh and human self-sufficiency.

Death, then, as man's destiny, 'came by man' (1 Cor. 15.21); as a fate, if not as a biological fact (Paul never so distinguishes), it 'entered into the world . . . through sin; and . . . passed unto all men, for that all sinned' (Rom. 5.12). It overspread the total human situation and 'reigned . . . even over them that had not sinned after the likeness of Adam's transgression' (Rom. 5.14).[1] The universality of death as the destiny of man is thus not a natural fact like the mortality of the σάρξ. 'The body of death' is a terrible contradiction—for man as σῶμα is not made to belong to death. Death is an intruder in God's universe: it entered upon its reign over man from outside. It is one of 'the powers' which have got this age in their grip and 'now work in the sons of disobedience' (Eph. 2.2). It is 'the last enemy' to be abolished with the close and defeat of the Age itself (1 Cor. 15.26), because it represents the final denial of the life and love of God.[2] Consequently, to be human is now to be subject to a servitude (Rom. 6.16), a dominion (Rom. 6.9) at the hands of death. To

---

[1] *I.e.*, not in conscious knowledge of what they were doing (παράβασις). The consequences of having missed the mark of human existence (ἁμαρτία) follow even where a man is not fully aware of what that mark is. Adam, since he knew the will of God for man, is regarded by Paul as prefiguring humanity under the law, which was not given historically in the Jewish Torah till the time of Moses. The clause 'who is a type of him that was to come' seems best taken thus, in explanation of the difficulty that in the case of Adam alone 'transgression' was possible before the law. τοῦ μέλλοντος will then refer to Moses, or, generally, to 'man under the law'. Or perhaps it is neuter and means simply 'the future', 'what was to come' (*cf.* Col. 2.17; Luke 13.9; 1 Tim. 6.19). If it is taken to refer to Christ, the relative clause is no more than a device for resuming the main argument and must be taken closely with what follows. The argument of v. 14 then becomes purely assertive.

[2] θάνατος, death, is the end term of that separation from God which is portrayed in the other phrases that Paul uses to characterise the human situation, *viz.*: ἐχθρά, enmity, the twisting of the fundamental relationship between man and God (and consequently also of that between man and man) to a sterile antagonism, and ὀργή, wrath, the abandonment (*cf.* παρέδωκεν, Rom. 1.24) of society by God, to 'stew in its own juice', to reap the retribution of its own misdeeds.

die, for fallen man, is the sacrament and symbol of defeat by
death: physical expiration is the outward confirmation of being
in fact already 'dead' (νεκρός; Eph. 2.1). This is what gives it
its victory. So, the Christian who has already risen beyond the
power of death may 'sleep' (1 Cor. 15.51) (till the end of this age
finally breaks the consequences of evil), but he cannot be
triumphed over by death: 'O death where is thy victory?' (1
Cor. 15.55).

(2) With a share in the dominion of death over man is *sin*—'sin
reigned in death' (Rom. 5.21). It is the accomplice of death, the
agent which gives it entry into the human situation (Rom. 5.12).[1]
It is 'the sting of death' (1 Cor. 15.56); *i.e.*, 'death employed sin
to stab for itself an opening into human nature' (C. A. Anderson
Scott, *Christianity According to St. Paul*, 51). Consequently, men's
state is equally one of slavery to sin (Rom. 6.6, 17, 20). In essence,
indeed, sin is an act of human freedom, whose prime nature is
disobedience (Rom. 5.19). But it is something which has long
since got out of man's control. It is a symbol now not of freedom,
but of determinism. Like death, it has become an alien power
residing within the individual, denying him command of his own
actions: 'It is no more I that do it, but sin which dwelleth in me'
(Rom. 7.17, 20). It has its own law under which the self is a
prisoner (Rom. 7.23). It exercises the functions of king (Rom.
5.14) and lord (Rom. 6.14); it is a slave-owner to whom man has
been sold as a chattel (Rom. 7.14). In a phrase, all things have
been shut up 'under sin' (ὑπὸ ἁμαρτίαν: Gal. 3.22).

(3) If sin is the accomplice of death, the *law* is the instrument
of sin. As death comes 'through sin' (Rom. 5.12), so sin comes
'through the law' (Rom. 7.5). For it is by means of the commandment that sin obtains its ἀφορμή in man (Rom. 7.8, 11), the footing
or bridgehead that forms its base of operations for occupying
human nature. 'The power of sin', its capacity to induce disobedience, 'is the law' (1 Cor. 15.56). The law achieves this
because of its effect on the flesh. The σάρξ, as we have seen, is

---

[1] *Cf.* the similar expressive personification in Gen. 4.7: 'Sin coucheth at the door.'

not in itself evil or sinful. But it is essentially 'weak', and easily 'beguiled' (Rom. 7.11); it needs but the least 'occasion' (Gal. 5.13). It forms therefore, in the language of a later age, the *fomes peccati*, the tinder that only requires a flame. It is highly combustible, and susceptible of inflammation by the law, which excites the passions and causes sin to blaze to life (Rom. 7.5, 9). The psychological mechanism which this sets in motion (*vide* Rom. 7.7 ff) is not here our concern. The outcome is that man is in a state of bondage equally to the law, as he is to sin and the powers of death (Gal. 4.1-7; 5.1). He can be described as 'under' the law (Rom. 6.14; Gal. 4.21) just as he is 'under' sin. He is 'holden' by it (Rom. 7.6)—in its charge (Rom. 7.6) and ward (Gal. 3.23), subject to its curse (Gal. 3.13).

This whole process and state of man's triple enslavement is summed up in Rom. 7.11: 'Sin, finding occasion, through the commandment beguiled me, and through it slew me'—the law, leading to sin, resulting in death. The same sequence is to be found in Rom. 7.5: 'the sinful passions, which were through the law, wrought in our members to bring forth fruit unto death', the whole thing being possible because 'we were in the flesh'. For the σάρξ is that 'wherein' we are holden (Rom. 7.6), the seat and ground of this whole servitude.

It is, then, into such a situation that Christ came when He took flesh. The process of the redemption He wrought in it is seen by Paul as including three moments or stages. For the purpose of analysing and clarifying his thought, it is possible to work out how each of these stages is related in turn to the threefold slavery under which man stands—to the 'powers' of evil (represented, *par excellence*, by death), to sin, and to the law. But such an analysis must not obscure the fact that these three form a single interrelated complex of bondage and frustration.

(1) The first act in the drama of redemption is the self-identification of the Son of God *to the limit*, yet without sin, with the body of the flesh in its fallen state. It is necessary to stress these words because Christian theology has been extraordinarily reluc-

tant to accept at their face value the bold, and almost barbarous, phrases which Paul uses to bring home the offence of the Gospel at this point. Traditional orthodoxy, both Catholic and Protestant, has held that Christ assumed at the Incarnation an unfallen human nature.[1] This is not the place to debate the doctrinal issues that have been historically mixed up with this belief. There is no doubt that the discussion has been bedevilled by the unfortunate association of original sin with theories of (*a*) original guilt (which clearly could not be predicated of a sinless Saviour) and (*b*) biological transmission (believed to be broken in the case of Christ by divine conception). But if the question is restated in its Biblical terms, there is no reason to fear, and indeed the most pressing grounds for requiring, the ascription to Christ of a manhood standing under all the effects and consequences of the Fall. At any rate, it is clear that this is Paul's view of Christ's person, and that it is essential to his whole understanding of His redeeming work.

This first moment of complete self-identification with man's lost estate is worked out by Paul

(i) *In relation to the powers of death*. For Christ to take flesh meant that He took upon Himself 'the form of a slave, being made in the likeness of men' (Phil. 2.7). The reference here is not merely to Jesus' lowly status on earth. It means that, by assuming σάρξ, He accepted the position of being a δοῦλος (strictly 'a slave born') to 'the powers', in the likeness of all other men who are 'enslaved under the elemental spirits of the world' (Gal. 4.3). By voluntarily entering their thraldom, He passed under the dominion of death. He assumed a 'mortal body': the Son of Man, like

[1] Prof. Karl Barth, who devotes a long note to the subject in his *Dogmatik* I, 2, 167-9, can quote no writer on the other side until the nineteenth century. Despite its most disreputable ancestry (for which see also: A. B. Bruce, *The Humiliation of Christ*, VI), he has no hesitation in opting, as he believes with the New Testament, for the view that 'the nature which God took in Christ is identical with our nature under the Fall'. Christ, he writes, 'was no sinner. But His situation was, both from the inside and out, that of a sinner. He freely entered upon solidarity with our lost and wretched state. So and only so *could* the revelation of God to us, our reconciliation with Him, take place in Him and through Him' (*ib.*, 166). For a recent, though very brief, discussion of the matter, *vide*: D. M. Baillie, *God was in Christ*, 16 f.

every other fallen son of man, must die. Consequently, the powers, 'the rulers of this age', in due course put Him on the cross (1 Cor. 2.8).

And yet, while accepting to the uttermost the form and consequences of the slavery under which life against God is lived, never for one moment did He allow the powers authority over Him. He remained to the end their master. Paul never says that Christ *was* a slave, nor that He was 'enslaved', as he says of every other man. Under 'the form of a slave', the μόρφη δούλου (by which is intended nothing in the least docetic, but the most realistic description of the condition of fallen humanity[1]), Christ led a life of complete alignment with the will of God, 'becoming obedient even unto death, yea, the death of the cross' (Phil. 2.8).

(ii) *In relation to sin.* 'God sent his own Son in the likeness of sinful flesh' (ἐν ὁμοιώματι σαρκὸς ἁμαρτίας, flesh that belonged to sin: Rom. 8.3). Nothing apparently could be more explicit. But Paul goes yet further, in the astonishing phrase that God 'made him to be sin for us' (ἁμαρτίαν ἐποίησεν: 2 Cor. 5.21). Yet even in this total identification, he is again most careful in his choice of words. He never says that Christ was a sinner. In fact he joins this last statement with the most positive assertion that He 'knew no sin'—'knew', that is, in the intimate Hebrew sense of physical and spiritual union. Christ had no intercourse with sin, He gave it no entry into Himself. It is by disobedience that men are 'made sinners': Christ's life was one of utter 'obedience' (Rom. 5.19).

(iii) *In relation to the law.* By being 'born of a woman', and thus entering the sphere of the σάρξ, Christ was 'born under the law' (ὑπὸ νόμον: Gal. 4.4), *i.e.*, subject to its bondage. Now, to be under the law is to be 'under a curse' (Gal. 3.10), a curse issuing in death. Christ, therefore, accepted this too, 'having become a curse for us', even to its end of 'hanging on a tree' (Gal. 3.13). But again Paul's language is most carefully chosen. He does not

---

[1] *Cf.* A. M. Ramsey, *The Glory of God and the Transfiguration of Christ*, 54: 'μόρφη means real being in contrast with outward appearance.' He instances Rom. 12.2: 'Be not outwardly fashioned (συνσχηματίζεσθε) according to this world; but be ye changed in real being (μεταμορφοῦσθε) by the renewing of your mind.'

say that Christ was actually 'accursed', as his reference to Deut. 21.23 would lead one to expect; for the curse acquired no force over Him.

(2) By His death Christ, as it were, 'died out on' the forces of evil without their being able to defeat or kill Him, thereby exhibiting their impotence and gaining victory over them.

The only way evil ever wins victories is by making a man retort by evil, reflect it, pay it back, and thus afford it a new lease of life. Over one who persistently absorbs it and refuses to give it out, it is powerless. It is in this kind of way that Paul sees Christ dealing with the forces of evil—going on and on and on, triumphantly absorbing their attack by untiring obedience, till eventually there is nothing more they can do. Or, rather, there is one thing more—and that is to kill Him. This they do. But in the very act they confess their own defeat. For all they achieve thereby is to deprive Him, still inviolate, of the flesh, through which alone they have any power of temptation over Him. He thus slips their grasp and renders them impotent. The Resurrection is the inevitable consequence of this defeat; death could have no grip on Him, since sin obtained no foothold in Him. It was impossible that He should be holden of it.

This process Paul works out in relation to the same threefold thraldom under which humanity stands.

(i) *In relation to the powers of death.* In 1 Cor. 2.8, the ruling powers of this age are represented as having crucified the Lord of Glory in ignorance. If they had known who He was they would not have done it. They would have realised that in His case such action could be nothing but the sealing of their defeat. For all they achieved thereby was to strip Him of the flesh, their sole entry for attack or hope of victory. Though they had put Him to death, they had done nothing to Him. In fact, throughout, it was really He who had been the agent. His death was the symbol and sacrament, not of their action in defeating Him, but of His voluntary act in putting off the flesh. Now this latter is the very thing the sinner cannot do: for it is the flesh that has power over him and not *vice versa*. Jesus' action in dying is therefore the sign of His triumph over the powers.

This argument is presented most clearly in Col. 2.15.[1] In the R.V. this verse runs: 'Having put off from himself the principalities and powers, he made a show of them openly, triumphing over them in it' (*i.e.*, the cross). But it can also be translated with the R.V.M. and many of the Latin fathers: 'Having put off from himself (his body), he made a show of the principalities . . .', etc. ἀπεκδυσάμενος (*sc.* τὴν σάρκα) then means 'having stripped' (in our intransitive sense of 'undressed').[2] It is through the σάρξ that death and its forces have control over human nature. The dying Jesus, like a king, divests Himself of that flesh, the tool and medium of their power, and thereby exposes them to ridicule for their Pyrrhic victory. From that moment death has no further dominion over Him (Rom. 6.9). Thenceforth the forces of evil are in the process of annihilation (1 Cor. 2.6).

That this is the right interpretation of this Colossians passage is confirmed by similar expressions which will come up for consideration shortly, and also by an earlier verse from the same context, namely, Col. 2.11: 'Ye were also circumcised with a circumcision not made with hands, in the putting off of the body of the flesh, in the circumcision of Christ.' The immediate concern of this passage is with the stripping off of the σάρξ by the Christian disciple (see below p. 43). But this is a process possible to him only because it is a sharing in what has already been done by Christ on the cross. Jesus' death can be called His 'circumcision'[3] because the Crucifixion was the real and complete laying aside of the flesh of which circumcision is the partial symbol. The metaphor makes sense only if Paul understood the death of Christ as

[1] The interpretation of this passage, and much else in this chapter, I owe to the admirable discussion of the death of Christ in C. A. Anderson Scott's *Christianity According to St. Paul.*
[2] ἐνδύεσθαι (except where it relates to armour: 1 Thess. 5.8; Eph. 6.11, 14) and ἀπεκδύεσθαι always in Paul take as their object the body or its equivalent (*cf.* p. 63 below). In 2 Cor. 5.3 f, ἐνδυσάμενοι and ἐκδύσασθαι are used in a similar intransitive way.
[3] *Cf.* Jesus' own description of His death as His 'baptism' (Mark 10.38 f; Luke 12.50).

essentially 'the putting right off' of His flesh-body. The reinforced compounds ἀπέκδυσις and ἀπεκδύεσθαι were in all probability coined by Paul to describe this unique process.

Anderson Scott thinks (*op. cit.*, 36-7) that Eph. 4.21 f contains a similar allusion. He connects the difficult phrase, 'as the truth is in Jesus', with the words that follow it, and translates: 'That, as was actually the case with Jesus, ye put off the old man and put on the new'.[1]

(ii) *In relation to sin.* By 'becoming sin for us', Christ accepted the 'end' of sin, which is death (Rom. 6.21). But whereas all other men die '*through* sin' (Rom. 5.12), 'the death that he died, he died *unto* sin, once' (Rom. 6.10). He died 'out on it'; He left it helpless. He accepted death at its hands; but this could not be for Him, as for the others, the confirmation of previous defeat and the seal of separation from God. Hence, His death was no victory for sin, but, on the contrary, the triumphant moment of His release from its power to hurt Him.[2]

Paul expresses the same thing in a forensic metaphor in Rom. 8.3. In Christ, he says, God 'condemned sin in the flesh'— κατέκρινεν, gave judgment against it. Seeing that Christ was 'in the flesh', sin puts in its usual claim to possess Him, as one of its subjects. But He has not become subjected to it: in this instance alone man is adjudged not to be the property of the claimant. The claim is negatived, and sin is put out of court (*cf.* C. H. Dodd, *Romans, ad loc.*).

(iii) *In relation to the law.* Christ as 'under the law' accepts its final doom of death. But by His death He redeems us from the curse of the law (Gal. 3.13). For in dying He exhausts its curse. Though the forces of the law may have joined in hanging Him on the tree, the law cannot ultimately kill Him. He accepts into

[1] For this use of ἀλήθεια as 'actual fact' he compares 2 Cor. 7.14: 'Our glorying . . ., which I made before Titus, was found to be truth', *i.e.*, it has corresponded with events, it 'has proved true' (Moffatt).

[2] *Cf.* Heb. 9.28: 'So Christ also, having been once offered to bear the sins of many' (Paul always prefers to this phrase the complete personal identification of 'being made sin'), 'shall appear a second time apart from sin' (χωρὶς ἁμαρτίας). This does not mean that this time He will be sinless—He was that before (Heb. 4.15) —but that He will be outside the power of sin to tempt Him, as no longer ἐν σαρκί.

Himself the worst that it can achieve. It destroys the body of His flesh. But it then has nothing more that it can do: 'for the law hath dominion over a man (only) for so long time as he liveth' (Rom. 7.1). Once He is no longer 'in the flesh', it is impotent. So, in Eph. 2.15, Paul speaks of Christ 'having rendered inoperative (καταργήσας) in his flesh . . . the law of commandments contained in ordinances'. The law has been removed from power over man by the stripping off of Jesus' flesh: Christ has 'blotted out the bond written in ordinances that was against us, which was contrary to us: and he hath taken it out of the way, nailing it to the cross; having put off from himself his body' (Col. 2.14 f).[1] The whole thing can be summed up in Rom. 7.4, 'Ye . . . were made dead to the law through the body of Christ'.

(3) What Christ has done in His flesh-body on the Cross has been through baptism, and must be in conduct, reproduced in the life of the Christian.

(i) *In relation to the powers of death.* 'Ye died with Christ', says Paul, ἀπὸ τῶν στοιχείων τοῦ κόσμου (Col. 2.20): 'out from under the elements of the world' is perhaps the nearest translation, in view of the manner of Christ's victory. For the exact process has been repeated in Christians by the act of baptism: 'Ye were also circumcised with a circumcision not made with hands, in the putting off of the body of the flesh, in the circumcision of Christ' (Col. 2.11). In Col. 3.9, he speaks of Christians as 'having put off (ἀπεκδυσάμενοι) the old man', exactly as in Col. 2.15 he had spoken of Christ 'having put off (his flesh)'. So, to quote Eph. 4.21 again, he exhorts his converts to live out the truth of their life in

---

[1] I have retained the R.V. rendering here, though convinced that τὸ . . . χειρόγραφον τοῖς δόγμασιν cannot mean 'the bond written in ordinances'. What Paul is saying is now erased is our *subscription to* the ordinances. (The dative is implied in the action of the verb.) The χειρόγραφον is our written agreement to keep the law, our certificate of debt to it (for the technical term, *cf.* J. H. Moulton and G. Milligan, *Vocabulary of New Testament Greek*). This, which stood in our name (καθ' ἡμῶν) since the day when the people of Israel first made their solemn act of assent to the commandments (Exod. 24.3; Deut. 27.14-26), has since proved a bond held up against us (ὑπεναντίον ἡμῖν) to prove our guilt. It is this bond, representing the power which the law has over us, rather than the law itself, which Paul now sees as 'nailed'. In Eph. 2.15 he uses the word καταργεῖν of the law itself (as he refused to in Rom. 3.31); but it is the law, not as the will of God, but as the symbol of 'enmity', that he has in mind.

43

Christ, 'that as was actually the case with Jesus, ye put off the old man and put on the new'. For 'brethren, we are debtors, not to the flesh, to live after the flesh; for if ye live after the flesh, ye must die; but if by the Spirit ye mortify the deeds of the body (*i.e.*, the σάρξ), ye shall live' (Rom. 8.12 f). This follows because with the flesh is put off the servitude to the powers of death. The Christian is delivered 'out of (ἐκ) this body of death'. He is removed from the sphere in which death has property rights over him: he is 'free from the law of . . . death' (Rom. 8.2).

(ii) *In relation to sin.* Again, Christians are those who have repeated in their flesh the process of the Cross. 'Our old man was crucified with him, that the body of sin might be done away, so that we should no longer be in bondage to sin' (Rom. 6.6); 'they that are of Jesus Christ have crucified the flesh with the passions and lusts thereof' (Gal. 5.24). Just as Christ died 'unto sin' rather than 'through sin', so Christians are men who at baptism 'died unto sin' (Rom. 6.2). Consequently, they must reckon themselves now 'dead unto sin' (Rom. 6.11). From this follows the exhortation, 'Let not sin therefore reign in your mortal body, that ye should obey the lusts thereof' (Rom. 6.12). 'Sin shall not have dominion over you' (Rom. 6.14), for you have been 'made free from sin' (Rom. 6.18, 22; 8.2).

The same forensic metaphor is in this connection used by Paul of the Christian that he applies to Christ. 'He that hath died is justified from sin' (ἀπὸ τῆς ἁμαρτίας: Rom. 6.7)—'a dead man has his quittance from any claim that sin can make against him' (Sanday and Headlam, *Romans, ad loc.*). Once a man is out of the sphere of the σάρξ, he can no longer be arraigned.[1]

(iii) *In relation to the law.* Once more, just as 'the crucified body of Christ made you dead to the law' (Rom. 7.4, Moffatt), so the same process has been repeated in the Christian: 'I . . . died unto

---

[1] There is an interesting parallel to Paul's argument in 1 Pet. 4.1 f: 'Forasmuch then as Christ suffered in the flesh (παθόντος σαρκί = the Pauline "died to the flesh"), arm ye yourselves also with the same mind; for he that hath suffered in the flesh (died to the flesh) hath ceased from sin (*i.e.*, has release from its power over him), that ye no longer should live the rest of your time in the flesh to the lusts of men, but to the will of God.'

the law. . . . I have been crucified with Christ' (Gal. 2.19 f). The logic of this rests on the principle already quoted, that 'the law has hold over a person only during his lifetime' (Rom. 7.1, Moffatt); and Christians are dead people. 'We have been discharged from the law, having died to that wherein we were holden (Rom. 7.6). Like Christ, the Christian has died to the law, by the putting off of the flesh. Consequently he is not 'under the law' (Gal. 5.18); he is free from the law which issues in sin and death (Rom. 8.2), and if this is so, asks Paul, 'if ye died with Christ from the rudiments of the world, why . . . do ye subject yourselves to ordinances?' (Col. 2.20). 'With freedom did Christ set us free: stand fast therefore, and be not entangled again in a yoke of bondage' (Gal. 5.1).

The whole work of Christ in redemption can be summed up for Paul in the words: 'You, being in time past alienated and enemies in your mind in your evil works, yet now hath he reconciled *in the body of his flesh through death*' (ἐν τῷ σώματι τῆς σαρκὸς αὐτοῦ διὰ τοῦ θανάτου: Col. 1.21 f; *cf.* Eph. 2.15 f). Both the Incarnation and the Cross are necessary: first, the complete identification in the body of His flesh with the whole mass of sin and death; and, secondly, the stripping off of this body, in the power of an obedience perfect unto death, whereby the forces of evil are deprived of assault and exposed to ridicule.

It is this same process of identification and death, of incorporation and crucifixion, that Paul sees now as possible and obligatory for Christians. There is, indeed, no difficulty about the identification with the body of death: that is already only too solid. But how *can* Christians die to the flesh—the very action that men under its slavery cannot command?

Up till now, we have used expressions like 'as Christ . . . so Christians', as though the thing were a matter of imitation. But that is very far from being the whole truth for Paul. Indeed, if it were, he would have really no gospel of salvation at all. There would be nothing to join together what has been done for us with what has to be done in us. It is, indeed, precisely here that the weak spot of so many doctrines of the Atonement is apparent; and this is the reason why thousands fail to see any connection or relevance between the events in Palestine long ago and the changing of their own lives to-day.

But Paul, of all the New Testament writers, stands least open to this charge. The way in which he bridges the gap is of the greatest importance for his theology. Moreover, it is of crucial significance also for his doctrine of the body.

If one examines the phrases whereby Paul extends the death of Christ to the dying of the individual, it becomes apparent that they presuppose a nexus not of example but of something that can be expressed only by a variety of prepositions.

Thus, it is '*in* the body of his flesh through death' that Christians have been 'reconciled' (Col. 1.21 f), 'in the circumcision of Christ' that they 'were also circumcised' (Col. 2.11). It is 'in Christ Jesus' that men are 'made nigh' (Eph. 2.13) and possess 'life' (Rom. 6.11, 23; 8.2). It is 'in Christ' that they have 'redemption' (Rom. 3.24; Col. 1.14; Eph. 1.7) and 'forgiveness' (Col. 1.14; Eph. 1.7; 4.32), that they are 'justified' (Gal. 2.17), 'sanctified' (1 Cor. 1.2), 'made alive' (1 Cor. 15.22), and, indeed, that the whole process of salvation takes place (Eph. 2.6; ἐν Χριστῷ governing the complete sentence retrospectively). It is '*with* Christ' that Christians 'died . . . from the rudiments of the world' (Col. 2.20; *cf*. Rom. 6.8), that their 'old man was crucified' (Rom. 6.6; *cf*. Gal. 2.20; Rom. 8.17), that they were buried (Rom. 6.4; Col. 2.12), raised (Col. 2.12; 3.1; Eph. 2.6), quickened (Col. 2.13; Eph. 2.5), exalted (Eph. 2.6) and trust to be glorified (Rom. 8.17). It is '*through*' the Lord Jesus Christ, says Paul, that 'the world hath been crucified to me and I unto the world' (Gal. 6.14, R.V.M.; *cf*. Rom. 7.4). It is those who are '*of* Christ Jesus' that 'have crucified the flesh with the passions and lusts thereof' (Gal. 5.24); it is those who were baptised '*into*' Him who 'were baptised into his death' (Rom. 6.3) and 'did put on Christ' (Gal. 3.27).

Now all these phrases depend for their understanding on a single assumption and mean nothing without it. It is the assumption that *Christians have died in, with and through the crucified body of the Lord* (have a share, that is, in the actual death that He died unto sin historically, 'once for all' (Rom. 6.10, R.V.M.)) *because, and only because, they are now in and of His body in the 'life that he liveth unto God', viz., the body of the Church.* It is only by baptism into Christ, that is 'into (the) one body' (1 Cor. 12.13), only by an actual 'participation in the body of Christ' (1 Cor. 10.16, R.V.M.), that a man can be saved through His body on the Cross. The Christian, because he is in the Church and united with Him in the sacraments, is part of Christ's body so literally that all that happened in and through that body in the flesh can be repeated in and through him now. This connection comes to clearest expression in Rom. 7.4: 'Wherefore, my brethren, ye also were made dead to the law *through the body of Christ*; that ye should be joined to another, even to him who was raised from the dead.' Here the words in italics mean *both* 'through the fact that Christ in His flesh-body died to the law' *and* 'through the fact that you now are joined to and are part of that body'.

How closely these two uses (one can hardly say 'senses') of the word 'body' are connected for Paul may be seen by taking together Col. 1.21 f ('you . . . hath he reconciled in the body of his flesh through death') and its doublet in Eph. 2.15 f ('that he . . . might reconcile them both in one body unto God through the cross'). The context of these two passages each supplies the use that is lacking respectively in the other, and shows that the Pauline gospel depends on both of them being held securely together.

Indeed, we may say with Dr. Schweitzer that 'all attempts to distinguish in the relevant passages between the personal [historical] and the mystical body of Christ are inevitably doomed to failure. The obscurity was intended by Paul. The body of Christ is no longer thought of by him as an isolated entity, but as the point from which the dying and rising again, which began with Christ, passes over to the Elect who are united with him' (*The Mysticism of Paul the Apostle*, 118). 'The body nailed to the Cross was, therefore, in this sense the new organism of the One Man in whom we all die (2 Cor. 5.14)' (L. S. Thornton, *The Common Life in the Body of Christ*, 295).

Thus, the concept of the Body supplies the lynch-pin of Paul's thought. For we are here at the very pivotal point on which the whole of his theology turns, and by virtue of which also it is distinctive in the New Testament.[1] Moreover, the very cruciality of its usage here is of decisive importance for its interpretation. For if this is the point from which his doctrine of the Church as 'the body of Christ' grows and to which it constantly returns, then the interpretation which the word σῶμα here demands must govern our whole subsequent understanding of it. Whatever the linguistic source or sources may have been from which Paul brought that most characteristic of all his expressions, τὸ σῶμα τοῦ Χριστοῦ, it should be axiomatic that it has to be elucidated and interpreted, not primarily in terms of these sources, but *in terms of his own Christology*. The justification of this and its consequences must be left to the next chapter.

[1] The few passages in the rest of the New Testament which at first sight come near to Paul's teaching on the body all stop short at this point: they make no connection between the body of Christ crucified and that of the Church. The Pauline flavour of 1 Pet. 4.1 has already been noticed: 'Forasmuch then as Christ suffered in the flesh, arm ye yourselves also with the same mind; for he that hath suffered in the flesh hath ceased from sin.' But the exhortation to imitate is not grounded, as by Paul, in the fact that *in* the suffering body of Christ Christians have already died to the flesh. The same applies to 1 Pet. 2.21-4: 'Christ also suffered for you, leaving you an example that ye should follow in his steps: . . . who his own self bare our sins in his body upon the tree, that we, having died unto sins, might live unto righteousness.' It is instructive to compare this and its sequel in the next verse, 'for ye were going astray like sheep; but are now returned unto the Shepherd and Bishop of your souls', with the similar passage in Eph. 2.12-16: 'Ye were at that time separate from Christ, aliens from the commonwealth of Israel. . . . But now in Christ Jesus ye that once were far off are made nigh in the blood of Christ . . .; that he might create *in himself* of the twain one new man, so making peace; and might reconcile them both *in one body* unto God through the cross.' It is essentially the same teaching, but Peter knows no doctrine of Christ's body the Church.

Again, in Heb. 10.10, 'we have been sanctified through the offering of the body of Jesus Christ once for all', there is nothing that can be called a theology of the body. In fact, the occurrence of the word σῶμα in this passage at all is probably governed by its appearance in the LXX version of Psalm 40.7 which the author has quoted in v. 5. His theology is worked out in terms of the *blood* (10.19-22; *cf.* 9.22). αἵματος not σώματος is in fact the Western reading in 10.10.

In John 2.21, 'the temple of his body' refers to the body of Jesus' flesh now glorified. There is no suggestion of its identification with the Church.

CHAPTER THREE

THE BODY OF THE RESURRECTION

(1) THE EXTENSION OF THE INCARNATION

'WHEREFORE, my brethren, ye also were made dead to the law through the body of Christ; that ye should be joined to another, even to him who was raised from the dead, that we might bring forth fruit unto God' (Rom. 7.4). This verse, perhaps, more than any other could stand as a summary of the whole of Pauline theology. The first clause of it we have already considered. The subject of this chapter is the second—namely, the Christian's participation in the resurrection body of the Lord.

The title of the chapter has been deliberately framed, so as to bring together under a single treatment the Pauline doctrine of what is usually differentiated as the glorified, the mystical and the eucharistic body of Christ, along with the Christian's hope of the resurrection and renewal of his own body. The clue to the unity of Paul's thought at this point lies in the connection, made in the verse quoted above, of all this with the flesh-body of the incarnate Jesus. For the whole of his doctrine of the Church is an extension of his Christology.

This fact, and with it the inextricable relatedness of all Paul's uses of σῶμα, has been obscured by the very success of his description of the Church as the Body of Christ. The use of the word 'body' to mean a group of people is to us so familiar—'corporate' in fact now means 'social' and nothing else—that it is easy to forget that it was quite unfamiliar, if not entirely unknown, to the people to whom Paul was writing.[1] Further, it is important

---

[1] Prof. A. M. Ramsey goes so far as to say: 'Such a use is never found in Christian literature, or in the Septuagint, or in the papyri' (*The Gospel and the Catholic Church*, 35). There are, of course, many instances, particularly in Stoic writers, of the state or the universe being compared to a body (*cf.* W. L. Knox, *Journal of Theological Studies*, 39 (1938), 243-6). But the point of this simile lies precisely in the fact that the thing in question is likened to an *organism*. The word 'body' does not *itself* mean a society or collection.

Caution, however, is needed. There is a certain amount of evidence that the

to recognise that the Apostle is not apparently conscious of making any innovation in his usage. It is naturally impossible for us to know how much teaching lay behind the epistles now extant. But he uses the language to four different churches (wherever the epistle 'to the Ephesians' may have been meant for), including two (Rome and Colossae) he had not visited; and nowhere does he have to justify his *terminology*, however startling may have been the content he put into it.

If we do not count 1 Cor. 1.13 ($\mu\epsilon\mu\acute{\epsilon}\rho\iota\sigma\tau\alpha\iota$ ὁ Χρίστος;), Paul first uses the language of the body in relation to the Church in 1 Cor. 6.15: 'Know ye not that your bodies are *members* of Christ?'. He appeals here to a conception with which he assumes the Corinthians will already be cognisant. Now, in this instance he is quite clearly referring not to a society but to a person, *viz.*, Christ. To say that individuals are members of a person is indeed a very violent use of language—and the context shows that Paul obviously meant it to be violent. It is not surprising that the content of the new wine stretched the old skin to breaking point, so that we now accept as commonplace the idea of a 'body corporate'. But it is of great importance to see that when Paul took the term $\sigma\hat{\omega}\mu\alpha$ and applied it to the Church, what it must have conveyed to him and his readers was (to employ a distinction which itself would have surprised him) something *not corporate but corporal*. It directed the mind to a person; it did not of itself suggest a social group. Hence, as Prof. A. M. Ramsey has well remarked, 'to call the Church τὸ σῶμα τοῦ Χριστοῦ was to draw attention to it not primarily as a collection of men, but primarily as Christ Himself in His own being and life' (*The Gospel and the*

word was already in use purely metaphorically in a collective sense. Thus in 60 B.C. Cicero sends Atticus the speeches he had delivered as consul and refers to them as 'hoc totum σῶμα' (*Ad Att.* II, 1.3; quoted, among other parallels from Josephus, by G. C. Richards, *Journal of Theological Studies*, 38 (1937), 165). It is interesting how the Roman lapses into Greek for an idea which, it is usually held, was expressed by the Latin *corpus* but not by the Greek σῶμα. The most notable instance is that cited by Prof. T. W. Manson (*Journal of Theological Studies*, 37 (1936), 385) from a fragment of the year 7/6 B.C., where it is used of a 'body' of Greeks. But, as Manson himself points out, Paul's usage is very different. The Apostle never speaks of 'a body of Christians' but always of 'the Body of Christ'. For him, at any rate, the word clearly referred to the organism of a particular person.

Catholic Church, 35). It referred as directly to the organism of Christ's person as his other language about 'the body of his flesh'.

Consequently, one must be chary of speaking of 'the metaphor' of the Body of Christ. Paul uses the analogy of the human body to elucidate his teaching that Christians form Christ's body. But the analogy holds because they are in literal fact the risen organism of Christ's person in all its concrete reality. What is arresting is his identification of this personality with the Church. But to say that the Church is the body of Christ is no more of a metaphor than to say that the flesh of the incarnate Jesus or the bread of the Eucharist is the body of Christ. None of them is 'like' His body (Paul never says this): each of them *is* the body of Christ, in that each is the physical complement and extension of the one and the same Person and Life. They are all expressions of a single Christology.

It is almost impossible to exaggerate the materialism and crudity of Paul's doctrine of the Church as literally now the resurrection *body* of Christ. The language of 'membership' of a body corporate has become so trite that the idea that the individual can be a 'member' has ceased to be offensive. The force of Paul's words can to-day perhaps be got only by paraphrasing: 'Ye are the body of Christ and severally membranes thereof' (1 Cor. 12.27).[1] The body that he has in mind is as concrete and as singular as the body of the Incarnation. His underlying conception is not of a supra-personal collective, but of a specific personal organism.[2] He is not saying anything so weak as that the Church is a society with a common life and governor, but that its unity is that of a single physical entity: disunion is dismemberment. For it is in fact no other than the glorified body of the risen and ascended Christ. 'We are members of that body which was nailed to the

[1] The description of Christians as 'joints' and 'ligaments' actually occurs in Col. 2.19; *cf*. Eph. 4.16. Prof. C. H. Dodd suggests 'organs' as the modern equivalent of μέλη (*The Meaning of Paul for To-day*, 154).

[2] *Cf*. K. Barth: 'Believers . . . are therefore, in their fullgrown and no way attenuated individuality, *one body, one individual* in Christ. They are not a mass of individuals, not even a corporation, a personified society, or a "totality", but The Individual, The One, The New Man' (*Romans*, 443).

Cross, laid in the tomb and raised to life on the third day. There is only one organism of the new creation; and we are members of that one organism which is Christ' (L. S. Thornton, *The Common Life in the Body of Christ*, 298).[1]

It is to be noted how uncompromisingly physical is the language in which Paul depicts Christians as going to compose the resurrection body of Christ. This is particularly clear in the verse from Romans (7.4) quoted at the beginning of this chapter. They have been 'joined to another, even to him who was raised from the dead'. The unity is much closer than the English words would suggest. For the metaphor, as the context shows, is one of sexual union, and its presupposition is that the relation of Christians to Christ is that of 'one flesh' (*cf.* Eph. 5.28-32): they are fused in a single *basar*. This union is as exclusive as that of man and wife. It is possible only if Christians have been utterly severed by death (κατηργήθημεν, Rom. 7.6) from their former cohabitation with the σάρξ. To go back to that is to break the possibility of being *in* Christ. Hence, Paul's vehemence against those who by receiving circumcision wed themselves again to the flesh and the law: 'Ye are severed (κατηργήθητε) from Christ, ye who would be justified by the law' (Gal. 5.4).

The same presupposition comes to expression even more clearly in 1 Cor. 6.13-20: 'Know ye not that he that is joined to a harlot is one body? for, The twain, saith he, shall become one flesh. But he that is joined to the Lord is one spirit' (*i.e.*, a single spiritual body as opposed to a single body of flesh). Here again the new corporeity supersedes, and is utterly exclusive of, the old. For the fact that it is a spiritual body does not mean that it is not physical. To such an extent indeed is the new union with Christ physical (the word 'joined' is again one of sexual union—

---

[1] *Cf.* A. M. Farrer, *The Parish Communion*, ed. A. G. Hebert, 80-3. Paul knows no distinction between the ascended body of Christ and His 'mystical' body. For God 'raised us up with him, and made us to sit with him in the heavenly places *in* Christ Jesus' (Eph. 2.6); *cf.* Eph. 1.20-3, 'He raised him (Christ) from the dead, and made him to sit at his right hand in the heavenly places . . . and gave him to be head over all things to the Church, *which is his body*'. One could heartily wish that the misleading and unbiblical phrase the 'mystical' body had never been invented.

κολλᾶσθαι; *cf.* Gen. 2.24, LXX) that immoral sex-relationships can destroy it. It is in their 'bodies' (v. 15)—as σώματα and not merely as 'spirits'—that Christians are members of Christ. There can be no suggestion that because a Christian has ceased to be 'in the flesh' physical relationships have been left behind or become indifferent. Rather, the σῶμα has now truly become itself —the expression of the Spirit rather than the tool of sin working through the σάρξ. Reversion to fornication sunders a Christian from the risen body of Christ, just as much as it would had he actually been married to Christ in the flesh.

The idea of the bride of Christ, which is intimately bound up with that of His body and members, first occurs explicitly in 2 Cor. 11.2: 'I espoused you to one husband, that I might present you as a pure virgin to Christ.' It is worked out fully in Eph. 5.22-33. Here again the unity between Christ and Christians is that of 'one flesh', and as in 1 Cor. 6 the doctrine of the Body of Christ arises in discussion of the most physical relationships of bodily life. Indeed, there appears to be a studied ambiguity in the opening description of Christ as 'the saviour of the body' (Eph. 5.23). In themselves the words must refer to the Church, but they are set firmly in the context of a man's relationship to his wife 'as to his own body'. Moreover, the phrases 'the saviour of the body' and 'Christ loved the Church and gave himself up for it' are remarkably parallel to those which Paul used in 1 Cor. 6 of the physical body, to wit, that 'the Lord (is, or, was) for the body' and that Christians in their bodies have been 'bought with a price'. In the same way as no clear distinction can be drawn between the flesh-body of Jesus and the body of His resurrection, so there is no real line between the body of His resurrection and the flesh-bodies of those who are risen with Him; for they are members of it.

The same connection between the resurrection body of Christ and the physical life of the Christians comes out in the course of Paul's discussion of the sacraments. 'He that eateth and drinketh, eateth and drinketh judgment unto himself, if he discern not the body. For this cause many among you are weak and not a few sleep' (1 Cor. 11.29 f). Likewise, in 1 Cor. 10.1-12, he sees as a type and warning to Christians the very physical fate visited upon those members of the Church in the wilderness who fell away. For they too had been baptised 'into Moses' (*cf.* Rom. 6.3: 'baptised into Christ') and eaten 'the same spiritual meat' (*cf.* 1 Cor. 10.17: 'we all partake of the one bread') and drunk 'the same spiritual drink' (also from Christ, 'the rock').

A similar quasi-physical understanding of sacramental relationships within the Body underlies the practice of vicarious baptism for the dead (1 Cor. 15.29). In the purely incidental and *ad hominem* reference which he makes to it Paul expresses neither approval nor disapproval. But Dr. Schweitzer's comment is just. 'The position', he says, 'is not that Paul had to make the best of a misuse of baptism among the Corinthians, drawn from the heathen Mystery-religions, but rather that it was only in consequence of his teaching about being-in-Christ and his view of the effect of baptism that baptism for the dead could arise' (*The Mysticism of Paul the Apostle,* 285 f).

At any rate there is no doubt about his responsibility for the directives he issues in 1 Cor. 7.12-14, which rests upon the same basic presupposition. 'If any brother', he writes, 'hath an unbelieving wife, and she is content to dwell with him, let him not leave her. And the woman which hath an unbelieving husband, and he is content to dwell with her, let her not leave her husband. For the unbelieving husband is sanctified in the wife, and the unbelieving wife is sanctified in the brother: else were your children unclean; but now are they holy.' On this Dr. Schweitzer again comments: 'The unbelieving partner, through bodily connection with the believing, has a share in the latter's being-in-Christ and thereby becomes with him a member of the Community of the Sanctified. Because the married pair belong corporeally to one another, the unbelieving partner becomes, without his or her co-operation, attached to Christ and susceptible of receiving the powers of death and resurrection which go forth from Christ. . . .

And similarly, children sprung from such a marriage belong to the Community of the Sanctified' (*op. cit.*, 128).

It is perhaps significant that Paul prefaces this last passage with the words, 'But to the rest say I, not the Lord'. Prof. Oscar Cullmann has shown in his article 'Κύριος as Designation for the Oral Tradition concerning Jesus' (*Scottish Journal of Theology*, June 1950) how 'the Lord' in such cases is equivalent to the tradition of the Apostolic Church viewed as the voice of the living Christ. The conclusion of these verses, then, is Paul's and not the Lord's, because it rests on a conception which was not part of the common stock of Apostolic Tradition. The theology of the *body* of Christ is his own peculiar contribution to the life of the Church.

(2) The Origin of the Doctrine of the Body of Christ

The question naturally arises, From where then did he derive it? The answers have been almost as various as the investigators. The main sources suggested have been:

(*a*) *Stoic* (*e.g.*, Traugott Schmidt, *Der Leib Christi*, 1919; W. L. Knox, *St. Paul and the Church of the Gentiles*, 1939; G. Johnston, *The Doctrine of the Church in the New Testament*, 1943).

(*b*) *Gnostic* (*e.g.*, H. Schlier, *Christus und die Kirche im Epheserbrief*, 1930; E. Käsemann, *Leib und Leib Christi*, 1933; R. Bultmann, *Theologie des Neuen Testaments*, I, 1948).

(*c*) *The Old Testament Concept of Corporate Personality* (*e.g.*, A. Schweitzer, *The Mysticism of Paul the Apostle*, 1930; A. R. Johnson, *The One and the Many in the Israelite Conception of God*, 1942).

(*d*) *The Christian Eucharist* (A. E. J. Rawlinson, 'Corpus Christi' in *Mysterium Christi* (ed. G. K. A. Bell and A. Deissmann), 1930).

(*e*) *Rabbinic Speculation on the Body of Adam* (W. D. Davies, *Paul and Rabbinic Judaism*, 1948).

Now it is not our purpose in the present essay to reopen this question of the external sources of Paul's terminology. There can be little doubt that the *form* in which he chose to express himself was on occasion influenced by several if not by all of these sources.

He used the language that lay to hand and does not seem to have been over-particular about where it came from. Indeed, the extent to which these various sources were mutually exclusive has often been greatly exaggerated by those concerned to prove their own thesis. In the hellenised Judaism of Paul's day it is very doubtful whether most people would have been interested, or able, to isolate the differing ingredients of a syncretism which had by then become thoroughly mixed.[1]

But, wherever Paul derived his *terminology* (and the important influence of language on thought is not of course to be denied), our concern here is with the doctrinal content which the term σῶμα was used to clothe and express. And our contention is that his doctrine of the resurrection body of Christ, under all its forms, is a direct extension of his understanding of the Incarnation. But how came it that this extension was made?

There is no doubt that Dr. Rawlinson is on firm ground when he draws attention in this respect to the importance of the Eucharist. In the first place, Paul himself directly grounds the unity of the Church as the Body of Christ in the sacramental loaf, itself already declared to be the Body of the Lord: 'Because there is one loaf, we, that are many, are one body, for we all partake of the one loaf' (1 Cor. 10.17; Rawlinson's translation, *op. cit.*, 228).

Moreover, the words of institution at the Last Supper, 'This is my body', contain the only instance of a quasi-theological use of the word which is certainly pre-Pauline. Paul himself is careful to say of the narrative in which he quotes them that it was among the things that he 'received of the Lord', which he 'also' (*i.e.*, in his turn) 'delivered' to his converts (1 Cor. 11.23). It formed part of the Apostolic Tradition in which he had been instructed. This statement is corroborated by the ocurrence of the words in the same form in the Marcan narrative, which Prof. Jeremias believes

---

[1] *Cf.* the conclusion of W. D. Davies' *Paul and the Rabbinic Judaism*: 'We close our study, therefore, with the assertion that it is wholly artificial to make too sharp a dichotomy between the Hebraic and the Hellenistic elements in Paul's thought, and that any Hellenistic elements which may be found in his thought do not imply that he was therefore outside the main current of first-century Judaism' (320).

to be not only independent of, but more primitive than, the account in 1 Cor. 11.23-5.[1]

Further, the grounding of the doctrine of the Body of Christ in the Eucharist does full justice to the emphasis on which we have insisted, namely, that σῶμα is to be interpreted *corporally*, as the extension of the life and person of the incarnate Christ beyond His resurrection and ascension. For Prof. Jeremias again has shown (*op. cit.*, 103) that σῶμα in the words of institution almost certainly translates the Aramaic *bisra* (Hebrew, *basar*). The whole phrase, 'this is my body . . . my blood' (more familiar as 'flesh and blood') means that Jesus is making over to His followers 'till He come' His actual self, His life and personality. In so far then as the Christian community feeds on this body and blood, it *becomes* the very life and personality of the risen Christ.

But does it? There is a jump here, from 'feeding on' to 'becoming', which is not explained. And it is a jump not taken by any of the other New Testament writers, all of whom must have been as familiar with the words of institution as Paul himself. However significant the Eucharist may have been for Paul's theology of the Body, it is surely clear that it is not a complete explanation. What was it within his own understanding of Christ that made him—and no one else—take this, at first sight, extraordinary leap from the Eucharist to the *Ecclesia* itself as the extension of Christ's human personality?

The clue, perhaps, is to be found in another passage (1 Cor. 15.1-11) where Paul quotes the Apostolic Tradition, very significantly adding to it his own contribution. His claim is that the resurrection appearance of Christ granted to him, albeit 'out of due time', is strictly parallel with that given to the rest of the

---

[1] J. Jeremias, *Die Abendmahlsworte Jesu*, 80-99 (esp. 94-8). The assertion of Käsemann (*Leib und Leib Christi*, 176) that Paul deliberately changed the Greek formula of institution from 'flesh and blood' to 'body and blood', and that therefore the Synoptics must be influenced by Paul, is quite gratuitous. This whole section is indeed the weakest of his book. In his concern to find Gnostic influence in the whole of Paul's doctrine of the Church he undertakes to interpret even the Last Supper without reference to any Jewish background. He admits somewhat ingenuously in a footnote (p. 174) that Jewish influences should be taken into account, but says that he is only following the line of his own book (!).

brethren. He also had seen the Lord in His risen body. He does *not* regard it as significant that to him Christ had appeared, not in the manner of the great forty days, but in His post-ascension form: there was between the two an essential identity and continuity of appearance, of body.

Now, when we examine the narratives of this appearance itself, we find stressed in each account of Paul's conversion how the heart of the revelation which came to him was the fact that the Church he was trying to stamp out was no other than Jesus Christ Himself: 'Saul, Saul,[1] why persecutest thou *me*? . . . And I said, who art thou, Lord? And the Lord said, *I am Jesus whom thou persecutest*' (Acts 26.14 f; *cf.* 9.4 f; 22.7 f). *The appearance on which Paul's whole faith and apostleship was founded was the revelation of the resurrection body of Christ, not as an individual, but as the Christian Community.* In face of this it would seem unnecessary to go further for an explanation of why the Body of Christ inevitably meant for him what it did. As Prof. Émile Mersch has put it, 'Since that day, when he saw Christ in the Church he was persecuting, it seems that he can no longer look into the eyes of a Christian without meeting there the gaze of Christ' (*The Whole Christ*, 104).[2]

(3) THE ONE AND THE MANY

Is it really conceivable that Jesus Christ can *be* many persons? That was the problem with which Paul wrestled, and, later, the conviction which we see him trying to impress upon his readers. For us, starting as we do with our conception of the Body of Christ as a society, the most pressing problem is how the many can be one. The multiplicity is obvious, the unity problematic. For Paul, the difficulty lies the other way round. The singularity

---

[1] Σαούλ, Σαούλ. The lapse into Aramaic for the spelling of Paul's name, found nowhere else, is some evidence that we have here an indelible personal reminiscence.

[2] This same lesson which had thus burned itself in upon him is transmitted by Paul to his converts in 1 Cor. 8.12: 'Thus, sinning against the brethren . . ., ye sin against Christ.' *Cf.* Gal. 4.14: 'Ye received me . . . as Christ Jesus', and the extension of the principle in Philem. 17: 'If then thou countest me a partner (κοινωνόν—*i.e.*, a partaker of Christ), receive him as myself.'

of Christ's resurrection body is taken for granted, just as it was by those who saw it on Easter morning. It is the fact that it can consist of a number of persons that really calls for explanation. So we find Paul opening his longest discussion of the Church as the Body of Christ with the words: 'For as the body is *one*, and hath many members, and all the members of the body, being many, are one body, *so also is Christ*' (1 Cor. 12.12). The unity of Christ, as of the human body, is his starting point. He then proceeds to show that the body cannot in fact consist only of 'one member', but must be 'many' (v. 14). The point of the verses that follow (15-21) is *not* that the different members must be united among themselves (the question of schism does not enter till v. 25, and then it is quite incidental to the passage), but precisely that there must be more than one member if there is to be a body at all.[1]

---

[1] We have here a good illustration of how Paul uses his 'sources'. It has often been noticed that the imaginary discussion between members of the body in these verses bears obvious resemblance to a fable depicting a quarrel for supremacy between the parts of the body, which had wide currency in the ancient world. Lietzmann refers to the story as having been traced back as far as the twelfth century B.C. (*An die Korinther I und II*, 3te Aufl., 62). It appears in its most accessible form in Livy II, 32.9-12 in the fable of Menenius Agrippa, and is a particular favourite of Stoic writers. Lietzmann notes this or similar ideas in Dionysius of Halicarnassus, Plutarch, Aurelius Victor, Valerius Maximus, Cicero, Seneca, Sextus Empiricus, Dio Chrysostom, Themistius, Josephus, Maximus Tyrius, Epictetus, Marcus Aurelius, and 1 Clement; to which should be added Xenophon (*Mem.* II, 3.18), Philo (*De Praem. et Poen.*, 19 (114); 20 (125); *De Virt.* 20 (103)), and the Midrash on Pss. 14.1 and 39.2 quoted by Strack-Billerbeck, *Kommentar zum Neuen Testament* on 1 Cor. 12.12 ff.

The fable as it is related by Dionysius of Halicarnassus (Antt. Rom., III, 11.5) is worth quoting in part. 'A commonwealth resembles a human body. For each of them is composite and consists of many parts; and no one of their parts either has the same function or performs the same services as the others. If, now, these parts of the human body should be endowed, each for itself, with perception and a voice of its own and a sedition should then arise among them, all of them uniting against the belly alone, and the feet should say that the whole body rests on them; the hands, that they ply the crafts, secure provisions, fight with enemies, and contribute many other advantages toward the common good; the shoulders, that they bear all the burdens; the mouth, that it speaks; the head, that it sees and hears and, comprehending the other senses, possesses all those by which the thing is preserved; and then all these should say to the belly, "And you, good creature, which of these things do you do?..."' Then follows a defence of the belly, as sustaining all, though it seems to do nothing but take in; and the same argument is applied to the function of the senate within the commonwealth.

Now, Paul may certainly have derived his language in 1 Cor. 12 (though not necessarily elsewhere) from these or similar sources. But the differences should be

Paul's argument is that the resurrection body of Christ *can* be articulated in diversity *without ceasing to be a unity*. All the members of a human body form one body *despite* their number. So it is with the person of Christ. The corporal unity of the glorified Lord is axiomatic: it is never a conclusion from the diversity. It is worth noting how the fact of unity, as the basic datum, always stands for Paul in the main sentence; the multiplicity, on the other hand, is expressed by a subordinate phrase or clause with the sense of 'in spite of'. Thus: 'The members of the body, *being many*, are one body' (1 Cor. 12.12); 'Seeing that we, *who are many*, are one bread, one body' (1 Cor. 10.17); 'So we, *who are many* (οἱ πολλοί, many as we are), are one body in Christ' (Rom. 12.5); *cf.* Gal. 3.28, 'All you (πάντες ὑμεῖς) are one man in Christ Jesus'.[1] There must indeed be multiplicity if there is to be a body—and it is observable how the great passages on the Body are precisely in contexts which stress and demonstrate the inevitable *diversity* of Christ's operations (1 Cor. 12.4-31; Rom. 12.3-8; Eph. 4.1-16). But the diversity is one that derives from the pre-existing nature of the unity as organic: it is not a diversity which has to discover or be made into a unity.[2]

The fundamental idea for which Paul is arguing may be viewed as a reversal of the principle familiar to the Old Testament that the remnant, or ultimately the one, can represent the many. This principle Paul sees was central to the divine operation under the

carefully noted. (1) We are in these writers dealing simply with a simile ('A commonwealth resembles a human body'). 'For Paul, however, this is not merely a simile, but a mystical truth' (H. Lietzmann, *ib.*, 52; *cf.* J. Weiss, in Meyer's *Kommentar*, 1 *Kor.*, 302): the Church *is the* body of Christ. (2) Paul's point is not to demonstrate the need for unity among the members, nor to prove which is the greatest, but to show that the body must be made up of more than one person—quite superfluous in the case of a commonwealth, most necessary in the case of an individual organism. The whole underlying conception is different.

[1] The consequence of this basic unity is drawn in 1 Cor. 11.17-34. Those who by their individualistic practices show that they have no 'sense of the body' (v. 29, Moffatt) cannot eat the Lord's supper and participate sacramentally in the body of Christ. What the communicant receives is Christ in His body, the Church; and the unity of this body is axiomatic.

[2] *Cf.* Eph. 4.3 f: 'Giving diligence to *keep* the unity of the Spirit in the bond of peace. There is one body, and one Spirit.' The word is τηρεῖν, to watch or keep an eye upon an independently established unity, not to keep up one that will cease to exist unless men create and foster it.

old covenant, according to which a vicarious minority, progressively reduced by sin, carried God's purpose for the whole world. The clue to this divine purpose he recognises to have been the principle of selection (Rom. 9.11). Out of all mankind Abraham was chosen to found, on behalf of 'many nations' (Rom. 4.17 f), God's People, Israel. Yet 'they are not all Israel which are of Israel' (Rom. 9.6). Isaac was chosen, Ishmael rejected (Rom. 9.7-9; Gal. 4.30), Jacob taken and not Esau (Rom. 9.10 f). The same principle was at work in the case of the remnant under Elijah (Rom. 11.2-4) and Isaiah (Rom. 9.27-9), till, finally, the true seed of Abraham had been narrowed down to the single man, Jesus Christ (Gal. 3.16): 'One died for all' (2 Cor. 5.14). But now, Paul proclaims, the principle of exclusion has been set in reverse. Henceforward, it is not the one who represents the many, like the Servant of Jahveh (Isa. 42.1, etc.) or the Son of Man (standing for the whole 'people of the saints of the most High', Dan. 7.13-27). Rather, it is the many who represent the one. 'For as many of you as were baptised into Christ did put on Christ. . . . Ye are all one man in Christ Jesus. And if ye are Christ's, then are ye Abraham's seed, heirs according to promise' (Gal. 3.27-9). The many, to whom no limit can be put either of race, class or sex (Gal. 3.28), now constitute the one. Abraham's seed, the Christ, is still one, as the promise required (Gal. 3.16); but it is a unity which is inclusive rather than exclusive, representative not simply vicarious.[1]

If we now ask how Paul conceives this inclusion of the many in the one, we find a great variety of expressions.

At times he assumes the fact of it as though to question its logic would be impertinence—for instance, in the abrupt summary of 2 Cor. 5.14: 'One died for all, therefore all died.'

Most often he is content to express it in the simple spatial metaphor of being 'in' (ἐν) Christ and Christ 'in' us.[2] The fact

---

[1] *Cf.* C. H. Dodd, *Romans*, 187; A. M. Ramsey, *The Gospel and the Catholic Church*, Chs. II and III; O. Cullmann, *Königsherrschaft Christi und Kirche im Neuen Testament*, 35 f

[2] The instances of this are far too numerous to quote. For a few of the more important, see p. 46 above. A. H. McNeile (*St. Paul*, 284-6) and A. Schweitzer (*op. cit.*, 122-5) give fairly comprehensive lists. *Cf.* the analytical table of instances quoted by F. Prat, S.J., *The Theology of St. Paul*, 391.

that he can use these two apparently antithetical phrases shows the organic manner in which he is conceiving this relationship. As Fr. Thornton well puts it, 'We are in Christ, not as a pebble in a box, but as a branch in a tree' (*op. cit.*, 144)—for there is a real sense in which the tree is in the branch. We are in Christ in so far as His life is in us. As Paul himself says, in a metaphor to be noticed shortly, we are σύμφυτοι with Him (Rom. 6.5), grafted into His stock. The opposite of ἐν Χριστῷ is χωρὶς Χριστοῦ, cut off from Christ (Eph. 2.12 f).

The variations which he makes on this spatial metaphor of being 'in' Christ also reveal how he thinks of it in terms of an organism, whether human or otherwise. 'Ye have put on the new man . . . *where* there cannot be Greek and Jew . . . but Christ is all, and in all' (Col. 3.10 f). Similarly, he speaks in Eph. 4.15 of 'growing up in all things *into* him, which is the head'.

This same phrase, 'into Christ', also occurs in Rom. 6.3, which is immediately followed by a long passage speaking of the relationship as a being 'with' (σύν) Christ. 'All we who were baptised into Christ Jesus were baptised into his death. We were buried therefore with him (συνετάφημεν . . . αὐτῷ) through baptism into death: that like as Christ was raised from the dead through the glory of the Father, so we also might walk in newness of life. For if we have become united with him by the likeness (literally, 'grafted into (σύμφυτοι) the likeness') of his death, we shall be also by the likeness of his resurrection; knowing this that our old man was crucified with him (συνεσταυρώθη), that the body of sin might be done away. . . . But if we died with Christ (σύν Χριστῷ), we believe that we shall also live with him (συνζήσομεν αὐτῷ)' (Rom. 6.3-8).

To us, the idea of being 'with' Christ conveys something more external than that of being 'in' Him. But almost certainly it did not to Paul. In Gal. 2.20 he combines it with what is perhaps the closest of all his expressions of identification with Christ: 'I have been crucified with Christ (Χριστῷ συνεσταύρωμαι); and it is no longer I that live, but Christ liveth in me: and that life which I now live in the flesh I live in faith, the faith which is in the Son of God,[1] who loved me, and gave himself up for me' (R.V.M.). Χριστῷ συνεσταύρωμαι: Prof. Mersch's translation, 'I am "con-crucified-with" Christ' (*op. cit.*, 130) perhaps gets the force of the verb Paul has invented. Time and time again (in a way in which he does not have to with ἐν), he coins strange new words with the prefix συν- rather than use the plain preposition. He clearly feels the painful inadequacy of language to convey the unique 'with-ness' that Christians have in Christ. We are 'joint-heirs with Christ (literally, of: συνκληρονόμοι Χριστοῦ); if so be that we suffer with him (συνπάσχομεν), that we may be also glorified with him (συνδοξασθῶμεν)' (Rom. 8.17); God 'quickened us together with Christ (συνεζωοποίησεν τῷ Χριστῷ: *v.l.*, ἐν Χριστῷ) . . . and raised us up with him, and made us to sit with him (συνήγειρεν καὶ συνεκάθισεν) in the heavenly places, in (ἐν) Christ Jesus' (Eph. 2.5 f; *cf.* Col. 2.12 f); 'The Gentiles are fellow-heirs (συνκληρονόμα), and fellow-members of the body (σύνσωμα; Mersch: "concorporate"), and fellow-partakers (συνμέτοχα) of the promise in Christ Jesus' (Eph. 3.6).

It is surely clear that for Paul to do or suffer anything 'with' Christ speaks of no external concomitance, like the P.T. instructor who says, 'Now do this with me', but of a common organic functioning, as the new tissues take on the rhythms and metabolism of the body into which they have been grafted.

The same is true of the next expression we must consider. In Gal. 3.27 and Rom. 13.14 (*cf.* Eph. 4.24; Col. 3.10) he talks of Christians 'putting on' Christ. Now, his other uses of this verb (1 Cor. 15.53 f; 2 Cor. 5.3) and its opposite, 'putting off' (Col. 2.15), suggest that he is thinking of Christ as a new body rather than simply as a new set of clothes. That this is the right inter-pretation is made probable by Col. 3.9-15: 'Ye have put off the

---

[1] ἐν πίστει . . . τῇ τοῦ υἱοῦ τοῦ Θεοῦ. The genitive is probably to be taken as both objective and subjective. The faith which Paul has *in* Christ is indistinguishable from the faith *of* Christ which has now been communicated to him as part of His body. *Cf.* Gal. 2.16; 3.22; Rom. 3.22, 26; Eph. 3.12; Phil. 3.9.

old man with his doings,[1] and have put on the *new man* . . . where there cannot be Greek and Jew. . . . Put on therefore . . . bowels of compassion, kindness, . . . [*i.e.*, of the resurrection body of Christ]. And let the peace of Christ rule in your hearts, to the which also ye were called *in one body*.'

Then there are other, equally physical, metaphors. In Gal. 4.19, Paul writes to his converts that he is again travailing with them until Christ be 'formed' in them, like an embryo. In Eph. 4.13, he speaks of Christians growing up into the full stature of Christ. A different image, though equally physical, is the one already noted by which he thinks of Christians as 'joined' sexually to Christ (1 Cor. 6.17; Rom. 7.4; *cf.* 2 Cor. 11.2) in the unity of a single flesh (1 Cor. 6.16 f; Eph. 5.28-32). This, as we have seen, is closely connected in his thinking with the relationship of 'limbs' to a body (1 Cor. 6.15; 12.27; Rom. 12.5; Eph. 5.30; *cf.* Eph. 4.16). Again, Christians combine to compose a single human organism (Gal. 3.28; Col. 3.10 f; Eph. 4.13).[2]

It is significant in this connection that the other important metaphor which Paul uses of the Church, namely of a 'building' or 'temple', never describes the Christian's relationship to *Christ* but always to God or the Spirit. Thus: 1 Cor. 3.9, 'We are God's building'; 1 Cor. 3.16 f, 'Know ye not that ye are a temple of God, and that the Spirit of God dwelleth in you? . . . The temple of God is holy, which temple ye are'; 1 Cor. 6.19, 'Know ye not that your body is a temple of the Holy Ghost which is in you, which ye have from God?'; 2 Cor. 6.16, 'We are a temple of the living God'. Of this temple Christ indeed is 'the chief corner stone', 'in whom each several building, fitly framed together, groweth into a holy temple in the Lord; in whom also ye are builded together for a habitation of God in the Spirit' (Eph. 2.20-2). The whole thing is

---

[1] *Cf.* Rom. 6.6: 'Our old man was crucified with him, that the *body* of sin might be done away.'

[2] This must govern the interpretation of the phrase 'putting on *the new man*'. This is not a better self which each person puts on individually. It is always a corporate entity, the one Man, the *Totus Christus*. Cf. Eph. 4.24 f ('Put on the new man. . . . Wherefore . . . speak ye truth . . . for we are *members one of another*') and Col. 3.10 f ('Ye have put on the new man . . . *where* there cannot be Greek and Jew . . .').

'in Christ', and the Body is spoken of as 'built up' (Eph. 4.12, 16). The Body of Christ is, indeed, the same as the building of, or from, God (see below p. 76 on 2 Cor. 5.1). But it is probably no accident that Paul does not use the phrase 'the temple of Christ' nor designate the relation of Christians to their Lord as that of a shrine to its indwelling deity. For even that would be too external.[1] He always prefers expressions which indicate the relation of parts to the whole.[2] The Christian's calling is to a participation in the Son of God (1 Cor. 1.9). He can be known simply as a κοινωνός, a shareholder (Philem. 17; *cf.* συνκοινωνός, 1 Cor. 9.23). He actually has a part-share in the body and blood, the very self, of Christ (1 Cor. 10.16). Consequently, he cannot have κοινωνία with devils (1 Cor. 10.20 f), any more than he can have union with a harlot.

The final and apparently most satisfying way in which Paul came to express this unity of the Christian in Christ was to say, not so much that Christ is the body of which we are the limbs, as that we are the body of which He is the head or directing principle.

The idea of the headship of Christ is first adumbrated in 1 Cor. 11.3: 'the head of every man is Christ'. It is connected with the theology of the Body only in Colossians and Ephesians, where it appears in close association with the doctrine of the 'fulness' (πλήρωμα) of Christ.

The most striking expression of this complex of ideas occurs in Eph. 1.23, one of the most disputed verses of the New Testament.[3] It runs as follows: 'He [the Father] put all things in subjection

---

[1] In Eph. 3.17 he uses the prayer 'that Christ may dwell (κατοικῆσαι) in your hearts through faith', but he does not work up this idea into a theology of the relation of Christ to Christians.

[2] One can imagine Paul being perfectly happy with the Petrine image of Christians as 'living stones' (1 Pet. 2.5)—part of Christ, yes, and thus related *in* Christ to God; but not related to Christ as His temple.

[3] Recent discussions of this verse (and of others involved in it) include:
J. Armitage Robinson, *Ephesians*, 42-5, 152, 255-9; *cf.* 87-9, 100 f (1903)
W. L. Knox, *St. Paul and the Church of the Gentiles*, 186 f; *cf.* 160-7 (1939)
F. C. Synge, *Ephesians*, 14-16, 61-5 (1941)
L. S. Thornton, *The Common Life in the Body of Christ*, Ch. X (1941)
C. F. D. Moule, ' "Fulness" and "Fill" in the New Testament', *Scottish Journal of Theology*, March 1951, 79-86.

under his [Christ's] feet, and gave him to be head over all things to the church, which is his body, the fulness of him who all in all is being filled.'

It will serve for clarity if at this stage we leave aside consideration of the final and very contentious clause. The understanding both of κεφαλή (head) and πλήρωμα (fulness) has probably been unnecessarily confused by treating the two terms together, either as complementary (Armitage Robinson) or as identical (F. C. Synge). The ideas they convey are obviously closely related and tend naturally to occur in the same contexts. The terms are nevertheless independent and presuppose different metaphors.

The word with which κεφαλή must be taken is σῶμα. The head and the body are complementary terms, and every time the headship of Christ is mentioned in Ephesians and Colossians it is in the closest conjunction with His body, the Church (Eph. 1.22; 4.15 f; 5.23; Col. 1.18; 2.9f, 19). Christ is never spoken of as the head of things in general in a metaphorical manner, though His universal lordship is, of course everywhere presupposed. He is *head* only of His own resurrection body, in which Christians are incorporate.[1] How literally and organically this headship is regarded may be judged from Eph. 4.14-6: 'That we . . . may grow up in all things into him, which is the head, even Christ; from

---

[1] F. C. Synge starts from the position that the whole conception of the body of Christ is merely a simile, and that Paul is using σῶμα to mean not an organism but a community ('This latter usage he perhaps coined'). The grounds for rejecting such a view have already been amply considered. But it is interesting to note into what fantastic exegesis it forces him. Thus, '1 Cor. 12.27 means, Ye are, as a community of Christ, like a body. Similarly Rom. 12.5 means, We who are many (and yet a community) are like one body in Christ' (*op. cit.*, 64). It also renders him incapable of accepting the palpably physical use of the 'body' in Eph. (5.22-33) without violent and gratuitous emendation. In consequence, too, he cannot abide the notion that κεφαλή should literally mean a 'head'. His statement that 'There is no evidence that κεφαλή could be used in the first century as we use it in our idiom in such a phrase as "head of the state" ' (*ib.*, 15) is unbelievable after the evidence set out by W. L. Knox (*op. cit.*, 16 f). To say that it means the same as κεφάλαιον (summary), and therefore as πλήρωμα, is again groundless and improbable. Thus, one cannot say in Eph. 5.23 ('once again κεφαλή = κεφάλαιον') 'The husband is the summary of the wife'! In fact, in this passage he interprets κεφαλή as if it meant 'complement'— an impossible sense of κεφάλαιον, and one which he denies to πλήρωμα.

A propos of Knox's evidence, it should be stressed again that the title 'head' as it appears in contemporary literature is used purely metaphorically. Paul's usage rests on the conviction that there really *is* a body, the resurrection body of Jesus, of which He is the head and in which we are included.

whom all the body fitly framed and knit together through that which every joint supplieth, according to the working in due measure of each several part, maketh the increase of the body unto the building up of itself in love' (*cf.* Col. 2.19). The notion of 'growing up into the head', however crude physiologically, is obviously possible only to someone whose thinking through and through is in organic categories.

(4) CHRIST, THE CHURCH AND GOD

Closely associated, as has been said, with this final account of the relation of Christ to Christians is the language used by Paul about the fulness of God in Christ. The two conceptions are, however, different, both in origin and in meaning. It is almost certain that in the case of πλήρωμα we are dealing with a word that Paul deliberately took over for apologetic use from the Hellenistic circles to which he was commending the Gospel.[1] It has no connection with the image of the head and body, and it is a mistake to define it, over against the head, as its 'complement', *viz.*, the body.[2] The idea of the Church as the complement of Christ certainly gives a good, if violent, sense to Eph. 1.23 ('the complement of him who all in all is being completed'), in the light of which a similar interpretation can be given to Col. 1.24 ('I . . . fill up on my part that which is lacking of the afflictions of Christ in my flesh for his body's sake, which is the church'). It is not the boldness of the conception which should make us hesitate, but the fact that this use of πλήρωμα is very difficult to harmonise with the other instances of it, and of the verb πληροῦν, in the rest of Paul's writings, including the rest of Ephesians.

---

[1] *Cf.* J. B. Lightfoot, *Colossians*, 323-39; W. L. Knox, *op. cit.*, 163 f.

[2] So Armitage Robinson on Eph. 1.23. The use he quotes of πλήρωμα for the 'complement' of a ship or city is not a real parallel. The crew and population are what fill these and make them complete for their function. In this sense the complement of the head would be the brain, not the body. There is no evidence that πλήρωμα is used in the case of two mutually supplementary things. Thus, in Mark 2.21, it means a 'patch'—that which fills a hole and makes the garment complete for its function. It would be an unwarranted extension of this use to apply it to the other half of a pair of pyjamas!

In Col. 1.19 he says that 'it was the good pleasure of the Father that in him [Christ] should all the fulness dwell', *i.e.*, that 'the totality of the Divine powers and attributes' (Lightfoot), by virtue of which both for pagan and Jewish thought God filled the world,[1] should reside permanently and wholly in Christ (κατοικῆσαι). There was no need for the host of subsidiary powers through whom the Colossians believed the fulness of the Godhead to be dispersed and mediated: there could be nothing *outside* Christ.

In the following chapter (2.9) he goes yet further than this, and says that 'in him dwelleth all the fulness of the Godhead bodily (σωματικῶς), and in him ye are made full', or, 'ye are in him, being fulfilled' (Lightfoot). The present tense (κατοικεῖ), the consistent use of the word σῶμα in these epistles to signify the Church, together with the explanatory clause, 'ye are in him . . . who is the head', all make it probable that Paul means here that now, since the Ascension, this fulness of the Godhead is contained by Christ not simply in Himself but in such a way that it spreads over to those who have been incorporated in Him. The fulness with which Christ is filled by God is now filling those who are 'in' Him.[2]

In the light of this, let us turn again to Eph. 1.23. God gave Christ, says Paul, to be 'head over all things to the Church, which is his body, τὸ πλήρωμα τοῦ τὰ πάντα ἐν πᾶσιν πληρουμένου'. If one thing is certain, it is that the passive (or middle) πληρουμένου must be taken seriously. There is little or no justification for the A.V. and R.V. translation: 'the fulness of him that filleth all in all'. When Paul wishes to speak of Christ filling all things, he uses the active voice (Eph. 4.10). The only real question is *by whom* Christ is filled or fulfilled. Armitage Robinson says it is by Christians, the members of His body. He thus makes πλήρωμα, as we have seen, the complement of the head. More recently it has been

---

[1] *Vide* W. L. Knox, *op. cit.*, 163 f. *Cf.* Jer. 23.24 ('Do I not fill heaven and earth? saith the Lord'); Isa. 6.3; Ps. 72.19.

[2] *Cf.* John 1.14, 16: The Word was 'full of grace and truth' and 'of his fulness we all received'.

suggested by W. L. Knox (supported by Fr. Thornton) that the phrase should run 'that which is filled by him who is always being filled (*sc.* by God)' (*op. cit.*, 186). That is to say, the Church, as the body of Christ, is constantly receiving from Christ the complete fulness which Christ receives from the Father.

On balance, this second interpretation appears the more probable. In the first place, it fits exactly with the meaning of Col. 2.9 f as we have just expounded it, namely, that fulness with which Christ is filled by God is now filling those who are 'in' Him. Moreover, nowhere else does Paul speak of Christ being filled or fulfilled by Christians (for the interpretation of Col. 1.24, see below), whereas he frequently talks of the fulness which is in Christ being communicated to and filling the life of His members. Apart from the statement in Col. 2.10 that in Christ Christians are 'being filled', he prays, in Eph. 3.18 f, that they 'may be strong to apprehend with all the saints what is the breadth and length and height and depth, and to know the love of Christ which passeth knowledge', so that they 'may be filled $\epsilon\dot{\iota}s$ $\pi\hat{a}\nu$ $\tau\grave{o}$ $\pi\lambda\dot{\eta}\rho\omega\mu\alpha$ $\tauο\hat{\upsilon}$ $\Theta\epsilon ο\hat{\upsilon}$', up to the measure of (A. Robinson) the whole fulness of God.

The hope of Christians is nothing less than that the complete fulness of God which already resides in Christ should in Him become theirs. This can never be true of isolated Christians, but in the 'fullgrown man', in the new corporeity which is His body, 'the measure of the stature of the fulness of Christ' is theirs to attain (Eph. 4.13)—for the Father's decree is that the Divine fulness should dwell in Him, not simply as an individual, but $\sigma\omega\mu\alpha\tau\iota\kappa\hat{\omega}s$.

Such an interpretation is in line with the language, throughout the Pauline epistles, which speaks of Christians being 'filled' with some grace of Christ or of God (Rom. 15.13 f; Phil. 1.11; 4.18 f; Eph. 5.18; Col. 1.9; 4.12).[1] It also supplies a background

---

[1] In the last instance ('that ye may stand perfect and fully assured in all the will of God') the reading $\pi\epsilon\pi\lambda\eta\rho\omicron\phi\omicron\rho\eta\mu\epsilon\nu\omicron\iota$ has better support than $\pi\epsilon\pi\lambda\eta\rho\omega\mu\epsilon\nu\omicron\iota$; but the sense is much the same in either case, and its conjunction with $\tau\epsilon\lambda\epsilon\iota\omicron\iota$ links it with Eph. 4.13.

for the rather strange phrases about Christians 'filling' (*i.e.*, 'passing on the fulness of') the ministry and gospel they have received from Christ (Rom. 15.19; Col. 1.25; 4.17).

In this context let us consider Col. 1.24, which immediately precedes one of these phrases about 'filling' the Gospel. 'Now I rejoice', says Paul, 'in my sufferings for your sake, and fill up on my part that which is lacking (ἀνταναπληρῶ τὰ ὑστερήματα) of the afflictions of Christ in my flesh for his body's sake, which is the church; whereof I was made a minister, according to the stewardship of God which was given me to you-ward, to fulfil (πληρῶσαι) the word of God. . . .' Fr. Thornton rightly points out (*op. cit.*, 34 f, 305) that this passage should be considered alongside 2 Cor. 1.4-7. There Paul is saying that God 'comforteth us in all our affliction, that we may be able to comfort them that are in any affliction, through the comfort wherewith we ourselves are comforted of God. For as the sufferings of Christ abound (περισσεύει) unto us, even so our comfort also aboundeth through Christ. But whether we be afflicted, it is for your comfort and salvation; or whether we be comforted, it is for your comfort, which worketh in the patient enduring of the same sufferings which we also suffer: and our hope for you is steadfast; knowing that, as ye are partakers of the sufferings, so also are ye of the comfort.'

In both passages the presupposition is that the fulness of Christ's life, alike in His death and in His resurrection, now overflows into His body. In both cases also the direct concern is with the *distribution* within the body of the fulness thus continually being fed into it. They deal primarily with the relation of give and take between the members, rather than with the basic relationship of body to head which that distribution presupposes. So, in Colossians, Paul is not saying that he is making up anything lacking in the sufferings of the head; rather, that, of the overflow of Christ's afflictions which is ever pouring into the Church, he is glad to absorb in his flesh what should be the share of his Colossian brethren and to fill up in *their* stead (ἀνταναπληρῶ) the tax of suffering still outstanding to them. The whole thing is done for the sake of the Body, in which his especial stewardship as an Apostle is to fill out the word of the Cross for them, to be the means of channelling to them the fulness of life-through-death by which Christians are 'made full' in Christ (Col. 2.10) 'up to the measure of all the fulness of God' (Eph. 3.19).

This process by which the Church is gradually embodying the Divine fulness of Christ is further set by Paul within the total scheme of God's redemption, 'which he purposed in him unto a dispensation of the fulness of the times', namely, 'to sum up[1] all things in Christ, the things in the heavens and the things upon earth' (Eph. 1.9 f). Just as it was the good pleasure of the Father that the whole expanse of the Divine fulness should settle down in one man, Christ Jesus, so now that fulness is to be extended to incorporate every man, till all are brought within the One. In the Cross and Resurrection, indeed, the finished work of Christ was completed: all things have been reconciled 'through the blood of his cross' (Col. 1.20). Nothing can be outside the scope of that redemption, for 'He that descended is the same also that ascended far above all the heavens, that he might fill all things' (Eph. 4.10). Once and for all, God 'raised him from the dead, and made him to sit at his right hand in the heavenly places far above all rule, and authority, and power, and dominion, and every name that is named, not only in this world, but also in that which is to come: and he put all things in subjection under his feet' (Eph. 1.20-2). And yet, within that universal kingship, and to translate into moral obedience what is already a *fait accompli*, He 'gave him to be head over all things to the Church, which is his body, the fulness of him who all in all is being filled' (Eph. 1.22 f). What is complete in extent has to be made intensively effective: the circle of Christ's kingship must be filled in and filled out. And the agent of that filling is the Church; its function is to extend throughout Christ's redeemed universe the acknowledgment of His victory, 'to the intent that now unto the principalities and the

---

[1] ἀνακεφαλαιώσασθαι (*n. b.* the aorist of a single finished act) is derived from κεφάλαιον, a summary, not directly from κεφαλή, head. For Paul, Christ is κεφαλή only of the Body, the Church.

powers in the heavenly places might be made known *through the church* the manifold wisdom of God, according to the eternal purpose which he purposed in Christ Jesus our Lord' (Eph.3.10f).[1]

The Church is the covenant people of the new order. Hence the Body is the sphere of election: 'Ye were called in one body' (Col. 3.15); 'There is one body . . . even as also ye were called in one hope of your calling' (Eph. 4.4). The mode of entry into this covenant is baptism (1 Cor. 12.13; Gal. 3.27; Rom. 6.3; *cf.* Eph. 4.4 f). That which most decisively marks the Church off from the old Israel, and which stamps it as the eschatological community, is its common possession of the Spirit. So it is that: 'In one Spirit were we all baptised into one body, and were all made to drink of one Spirit' (1 Cor. 12.13); 'There is one body, and one Spirit' (Eph. 4.4). It is this Spirit—which Professor Cullmann has described as 'the anticipation of the end in the present' (*Christ and Time*, 72)—that enables those who are in the Body of Christ to participate already, in this age, in the resurrection mode of existence. Paul can call it the 'earnest' (2 Cor. 1.22; 5.5; Eph. 1.14), the 'firstfruits' (Rom. 8.23) of the life of glory. Yet, strictly speaking, the actual firstfruits is not the Spirit but the resurrection body of Christ (1 Cor. 15.20, 23: 'Christ the firstfruits'; *cf.*, Col. 1.18). The Spirit is the instrument[2] by which the substance of the resurrection hope, the risen body of Christ, becomes ours and quickens the bodies of those who are in Him: 'If the Spirit of him that raised up Jesus from the dead dwelleth in you, he that raised up Christ Jesus from the dead shall quicken also your mortal bodies through his Spirit that dwelleth in you' (Rom. 8.11).

[1] On the relation between the Church and the total *Regnum Christi*, *vide* O. Cullmann's monograph *Königherrschaft Christi und Kirche im Neuen Testament*. It is a pity he spoils an otherwise excellent treatment by taking the quite unsubstantiated view that the Church is simply the *earthly* body of Christ (28 f). This leads to the extraordinary conclusion in his *Baptism in the New Testament* that baptism is effective only in this life (34, 48). Contrast 1 Cor. 15.29 (baptism for the dead) and the (thoroughly Biblical) view he himself expounds in *Christ and Time* (239 f), that, by virtue of possessing (through baptism) the earnest of the Spirit, the dead in Christ are in a radically different position from those outside the Body. *Cf.* A. Schweitzer, *op. cit.*, 281-3, and below pp. 78 f.

[2] *Cf.* Gal. 5.5: 'We *by the Spirit* on the ground of faith wait for the hope of righteousness.'

(5) THE OLD BODY AND THE NEW

It is here that the connection becomes apparent between the Body of Christ and the renewal, resurrection and transformation of the bodies of those who live within it. 'If any man is in Christ there is a new creation: the old things are passed away; behold, they are become new' (2 Cor. 5.17, R.V.M.). By participation in the Body of Christ the powers of the age to come are released into the bodies of those who make it up, just as they were in the healing miracles of the incarnate Jesus. Hence the scandal that communicants should be 'weak and sickly, and not a few sleep' (1 Cor. 11.30): they are 'guilty of the body and the blood of the Lord' (1 Cor. 11.27).[1]

We saw before how Paul stresses that 'the body is for the Lord' (1 Cor. 6.13): it is meant to be that through which the glory of God is made manifest. But we saw also that Paul knows it is useless to preach this as a matter of natural ethic. For the body in fact is a body that belongs to the flesh, to sin. And because 'all have sinned' they 'go short (ὑστεροῦνται) of the glory of God' (Rom. 3.23). It is only on the ground that 'the Lord is for the body', that 'ye are not your own' (1 Cor. 6.19) but 'your bodies are members of Christ' (1 Cor. 6.15), that he can say 'glorify God therefore in your body' (1 Cor. 6.20). The glory of Christ's resurrection body can and must shine out of His members, 'reflecting as in a mirror the glory of the Lord' (2 Cor. 3.18). This is always the basis of Paul's ethic of the body. 'Reckon ye also yourselves to be dead unto sin, but alive unto God in Christ Jesus. Let not sin *therefore* reign in your mortal body, that ye should obey the lusts thereof: neither present your members unto sin as instruments of unrighteousness; but present yourselves unto God, as alive from the dead, and your members as instruments of righteousness unto God' (Rom. 6,11-13). 'I beseech you *therefore* (*i.e.*, on the grounds of the whole message of Rom. 1-11)

---

[1] On this theme, *vide* O. Cullmann's excellent essay 'La délivrance anticipée du corps humain d'après le Nouveau Testament' in *Homage et Reconnaissance, Recueil de Travaux publiés à l'occasion du soixantième anniversaire de Karl Barth*, 31-40.

. . . to present your bodies a living sacrifice, holy, acceptable to God, which is your reasonable service' (Rom. 12.1).

As a Christian, Paul's 'earnest expectation and hope' is that 'as always, so now also Christ shall be magnified in my body, whether by life, or by death' (Phil. 1.20). The suggestion that Christ might be magnified by his death is a reminder that, though it is to the resurrection body of Christ that Christians are joined (Rom. 7.4), this nevertheless is, and within this age must continue to be, at the same time a suffering body. Indeed, it is precisely by continuously 'bearing about in the body the dying (νεκρῶσις, literally, the "putting to death") of Jesus, that the life also of Jesus' can be 'manifested in our body. For we which live are always delivered unto death for Jesus' sake, that the life also of Jesus may be manifested in our mortal flesh' (2 Cor. 4.10 f; *cf.* Gal. 6.17; 1 Cor. 15.31; Rom. 8.36 f).

This paradox follows directly from the fact that the resurrection body of Christ is the body of His death, bearing the imprint of the nails. Being 'joined to . . . him who was raised from the dead' (Rom. 7.4) means being 'buried . . . with him through baptism unto death' (Rom. 6.4). To participate in the body is also to participate in the blood (1 Cor. 10.16), *i.e.*, in the sacrificial death of Christ. To 'fill out' Christ is to 'fill up' His 'afflictions' (Col. 1.24). Indeed, in the most obvious sense it is only in 'the likeness of his death' that we are at present united with Him: 'the likeness of his resurrection' lies in the future (Rom. 6.5). 'God both raised the Lord and *will* raise up us through his power' (1 Cor. 6.14; 2 Cor. 4.14). 'The sufferings' are our portion in 'this present time': 'the glory' waits to be 'revealed' (*i.e.*, at the last day) (Rom. 8.17 f; *cf.* 2 Cor. 4.17). 'We that are in this tabernacle do groan, being burdened; . . . we would be clothed upon, that what is mortal may be swallowed up of life' (2 Cor. 5.4; *cf.* Rom. 8.23).

And yet the 'newness of life' is ours, already in this age (Rom. 6.4): we are 'alive from the dead' (Rom. 6.13, 11). We were 'buried with him in baptism, *wherein*' we 'were also raised with him through faith in the working of God, who raised him from the dead' (Col. 2.12). God 'raised us up with him, and made us to sit with him in the heavenly places, in Christ Jesus' (Eph. 2.6).[1] Christians are as men 'translated' (Col. 1.13): Paul can even say that they have been 'glorified' (Rom. 8.30; *cf.* 1 Cor. 12.26 R.V.M.). Consequently, it is not merely that the afflictions are now, the joy hereafter: 'For as the sufferings of Christ abound unto us, even so our comfort also aboundeth through Christ. . . . And our hope for you is steadfast; knowing that, as ye are partakers of the suffering, so also are ye of the comfort' (2 Cor. 1.5, 7). Indeed, the suffering and the joy are not really different or exclusive things. 'Let us rejoice in hope of the glory of God. And not only so, but let us also rejoice in our tribulations' (Rom. 5.2 f). The Christian life is lived 'by glory and dishonour . . . as sorrowful, yet alway rejoicing . . . as having nothing, and yet possessing all things' (2 Cor. 6.8-10). 'I am filled with comfort and I overflow with joy in all our affliction' (2 Cor. 7.4); 'I rejoice in my sufferings for your sake' (Col. 1.24).

The tension between both these facts of Christian existence—the present possession alike of suffering and of resurrection, along with the future hope—is expressed most clearly in the great declaration of his purpose in life which Paul made towards the end of his days: 'That I may know him, and the power of his resurrection, and the fellowship of his sufferings, becoming conformed unto his death; if by any means I may attain unto the resurrection from the dead' (Phil. 3.10 f).

In 2 Cor. 4.16-5.10, he had already sought to relate the sufferings and the glory, the old body and the new. This is a most important passage for the understanding of the resurrection body, and must be studied in some detail.

Immediately prior to these verses, Paul has been speaking of the 'working' of the death and life of Christ within His Body, the

---

[1] *I.e.*, in fulfilment of the familiar Messianic expectation that the saints would sit with the Christ in His heavenly glory. *Cf.* Matt. 19.28: 'In the regeneration when the Son of man shall sit on the throne of his glory, ye also shall sit upon twelve thrones, judging the twelve tribes of Israel.' L. S. Thornton (*op. cit.*, 189-94) draws attention to the way in which the same word, παλιγγενεσία, regeneration, is used in the N.T. both for this and for baptism (Titus 3.5), which in principle effects it.

Church (4.12), and he concludes (v. 14) with the assurance 'that he which raised up the Lord Jesus shall raise up us also with Jesus, and shall present us with you' (*i.e.*, at His coming). He then goes on, in the passage under discussion, to give the grounds for this assurance. 'Wherefore we faint not; but even if our outward man is decaying, yet our inward man is (being) renewed day by day' (v. 16). This is exactly the same process of renewal that he alludes to in Rom. 12.1 f: 'Present your bodies a living sacrifice. . . . And be not fashioned according to this age: but be ye transformed by the renewing of your mind.' There is no contrast in these passages between the renewal of the 'body', on the one hand, and of the 'mind' or 'inner man' on the other (for the equivalence of the latter two, *cf*. Rom. 7.22). That with which νοῦς is contrasted (namely, 'the outer man') is the σάρξ (*cf*. Rom. 7.25) not the σῶμα. Man as σάρξ is, indeed, decaying, but man as σῶμα is being transformed continuously, in so far as he is a member of the Body of Christ, τὸ σῶμα τοῦ Χριστοῦ. For this Body is not among the things that are seen (τὰ βλεπόμενα, *i.e.*, the σάρξ) and belong to this age only (πρόσκαιρα), but is αἰώνιον, belonging to the age to come (v. 18).

It is in the light of this that the opening verses of Chapter 5 should be read. They simply carry the argument one stage further. 'For we know,' says Paul in v. 1, 'that if the earthly (ἐπίγειος: *i.e.*, fleshly; *cf*. Phil. 3.19; Col. 3.5) house of our tabernacle be destroyed' (that is, even if the decomposition of the σάρξ be carried to its limit in death), yet 'we have a building (οἰκοδομή) from God, a house not made with hands, eternal, in the heavens' —namely, the Body of Christ. Whenever Paul uses the word οἰκοδομή (except in the purely figurative sense of 'edification'), it means the Body of Christ, the Church (1 Cor. 3.9; Eph. 2.21; 4.12, 16), not an individual body.[1] Quite apart from this evidence,

---

[1] Armitage Robinson is clearly right in taking πᾶσα οἰκοδομή, even without the article, in Eph. 2.21 as meaning 'all the building', not 'each several building'. He argues the case at length in *Ephesians*, 70 f, 164 f, and is supported by Dr. Selwyn, 1 *Peter*, 289. The parallel language of the 'temple' (ναός) is also applied only to the Church (1 Cor. 3.16 f; 2 Cor. 6.16; Eph. 2.21), except in 1 Cor. 6.19, where the teaching already given in 1 Cor. 3.16 f concerning the whole Church is directly

the fatal objection to taking v. 1 as speaking of the individual resurrection body is the present ἔχομεν, 'we *have* a building from God'. Now, in 1 Cor. 15, and indeed everywhere else in Paul, including the rest of this passage, the final transformation of our existing body and the receiving of the new one is an event that must wait upon the *Parousia*. Until that time even those who possess the firstfruits of the Spirit have to endure in groaning expectation (Rom. 8.23). To suggest that we have a resurrection body ready-made to enter at the moment of death is to render unintelligible the inevitable prospect of 'nakedness' which Paul holds out for those dying before the *Parousia*.

Paul's discussion, to be sure, proceeds on the assumption that the *Parousia* is still likely to *anticipate* the death of those to whom he is writing. Hence (v. 2) the hope of the new body is expressed in terms of 'putting it on over' the present one; though the nagging afterthought presents itself (and this must be the meaning of v. 3): 'If, indeed, it *is* as clothed (*i.e.*, still alive), and not naked, that we shall be found (*sc.*, at the *Parousia*)'.[1] The depression from which even Paul himself suffers derives from the fact that we cannot be *sure* that this very fragile house of flesh will in fact last us until the *Parousia*, and that we shall not be required to face a temporary disembodiment. 'For indeed', to give a free translation of v. 4, 'we who are in this tabernacle do groan; we are oppressed, because we do not want to have to be stripped, but desire so much rather to be overlaid, so that the mortal (*i.e.*, the σάρξ) may simply be absorbed into life'.[2] Such is the natural horror

applied to each member of it. For a discussion of this and similar metaphors throughout the N.T., *vide* E. G. Selwyn, 1 *Peter*, Additional Note H. Dr. Selwyn thinks (*ib.* 286) that 'the striking word ἀχειροποίητον' in 2 Cor. 5.1 is echoed by Paul from Jesus' words about building another temple made without hands (Mark 14.58), which (as John 2.21 comments) must mean 'the temple of his body'. For Paul this body is the Church.

[1] The Greek is εἴ γε καὶ ἐνδυσάμενοι οὐ γυμνοὶ εὐρεθησόμεθα (*vide* H. L. Goudge, 2 *Corinthians*, *ad loc.*). For a parallel use of εἴ γε καί to introduce a qualifying afterthought, *cf.* Gal. 3.4. It looks as if εὐρίσκεσθαι is almost a technical term for being 'dis-covered' at the *Parousia*. Cf. 1 Pet. 1.7; 2 Pet. 3.14. This may throw light on Phil. 3.9.

[2] The Greek is βαρούμενοι, ἐφ' ᾧ οὐ θέλομεν ἐκδύσασθαι ἀλλ' ἐπενδύσασθαι. This is translated by the R.V., and indeed generally, as though it were οὐκ ἐφ' ᾧ ('not for that we would be unclothed'). Such a wrenching of the Greek seemed to me

with which the prospect of death can still weigh us down.

But, he goes on, as Christians, we really have cause for a good heart. For our surety rests, not in the flesh and its power to see us out, but in God ($\Theta\epsilon\delta_S$ is placed emphatically at the end of the clause in v. 5). And He has already 'wrought (or, worked) us into this very thing (*i.e.*, $\tau\delta$ $\sigma\hat{\omega}\mu\alpha$ $\tau o\hat{v}$ $X\rho\iota\sigma\tau o\hat{v}$)', and 'given us the earnest of the Spirit'. We have even now, as a first instalment of that 'habitation from heaven'[1] for which we long, a body which cannot leave us entirely naked. It is this present inclusion in the resurrection Body of Christ, the eschatological community, that is the ground ($o\hat{v}v$, v. 6) for our having 'confidence' in whatever state we may find ourselves, whether it be 'at home' in the old solidarity of earthly existence or not. For, alive or dead, we already have our portion, through the Spirit, in the new corporeity, which one day will be the only one.

It is a mistake to approach Paul's writings with the modern idea that the resurrection of the body has to do with the moment of death, and that it is the guarantee of our survival as distinct individual selves. As far as the latter point is concerned, we have already seen (pp. 15, 29) that the implication of 'the body' for Hebrew, as opposed to Greek and later Western, thinking is one of solidarity, not of individuation. Our survival (both now and hereafter) as distinct selves depends, for the Bible, not on the body, but upon the fact that everyone is called by God to a unique and eternal relationship with Himself. Paul sees the abiding foundation of individuality in each man's gift from God (1 Cor. 7.7, 17)

the only way to get sense out of the passage until Prof. C. F. D. Moule pointed out to me the excellent meaning which the strict order can yield. This confirms the interpretation given above of v. 3, which introduces the ground for depression of which this verse is the elaboration.

[1] 'From heaven', not 'in heaven'. The scene of the Messianic Kingdom and therefore of the body of glory, is a renovated earth. *Cf.* 1 Cor. 15.35, 'How are the dead raised? and with what manner of body do they *come*?', and Phil. 3.20 f, 'Our citizenship is in heaven; from *whence* also we wait for a Saviour, the Lord Jesus Christ: who shall fashion anew the body of our humiliation, that it may be conformed to the body of his glory.'

and each man's inalienable responsibility to Him (1 Cor. 3.13-15; 2 Cor. 5.10; Rom. 14.12). The resurrection body signifies, rather, the *solidarity* of the recreated universe in Christ. It is none other than the Body of Christ in which we have a share.[1] That is why it cannot be 'put on' in its completeness till He is all in all. Nowhere in the New Testament has the resurrection of the body anything specifically to do with the moment of death. The key 'moments' for this are baptism and the *Parousia*. Death is significant, not for the entry into the new solidarity, but for the dissolution of the old. This act of dissolution, even for the individual, is only partial; for the solidarity of the 'body of sin' is bound up with this age rather than with this earth. The dead, just because of their death, do not escape from the sighing and the patience with which we must all await the redemption of our body (Rom. 8.23-5). We do not have any advantage over them (1 Thess. 4.15) nor they over us: we are both 'together' in this matter (1 Thess. 4.17). As the author of the Apocalypse puts it, the cry of the dead in Christ still goes up 'How long?' (Rev. 6.10) while the powers of this age are yet active.

The resurrection of the body starts at baptism,[2] when a Christian becomes 'one Spirit' (*i.e.*, one spiritual body) with the Lord (1 Cor. 6.17), and 'puts on (the body of) Christ' (Gal. 3.27), 'the new man', which 'hath been created' (Eph. 4.24) and 'is being renewed . . . after the image of him that created him' (Col. 3.10). Baptism begins the substitution of the solidarity of one body by that of

---

[1] There is therefore no ultimate distinction between the individual resurrection body and the one resurrection Body, any more than one can isolate the present individual organism theologically (or, for that matter, scientifically) from the whole 'body' of creation. Paul, of course, is sometimes regarding this solidarity as a whole ($\sigma\tilde{\omega}\mu\alpha$) and sometimes from the point of view of the individuals composing it ($\sigma\acute{\omega}\mu\alpha\tau\alpha$) (*cf.*, *e.g.*, Rom. 8.11 and 8.23). But the hardening of this into an absolute distinction, and the consequent distortion of Paul's thought, has been influenced by the fear of personal absorption, against which the inviolable 'frontier' of the body has been held to be the safeguard. But, to the Hebrew, individuality is not in the least endangered by saying that, as $\sigma\tilde{\omega}\mu\alpha$, man is 'part of one stupendous whole'. In fact Paul deliberately substitutes a new solidarity for the old, without in any way undermining the fact of individuality.

[2] *Cf.* the direct connection between baptism and the eschatological 'glory' in Eph. 5.26 f.

79

another (*cf.* Rom. 6.3, 6, 12). Each time this act takes place[1] the redemption of the old mortality is extended. A new part of the σῶμα of creation, which is made 'for the Lord', begins its release from 'the bondage of corruption' (Rom. 8.21), to which its identification with the σάρξ has doomed it. Its ultimate destiny, by incorporation into the Body of Christ, is transformation from being a natural body to become a σῶμα πνευματικόν (1 Cor.15.44); from a body that is merely 'a living soul',[2] 'earthy' and 'mortal', to one quickened by the life-giving Spirit of the last, or heavenly, Adam (Rom. 8.11; 1 Cor. 15.45-9); from a body of 'humiliation' and 'dishonour', to one wholly refashioned to 'the body of his glory, according to the working whereby he is able even to subject all things unto himself' (Phil. 3.21; 1 Cor. 15.43; *cf.* Col. 3.4). Consequently, the process of redemption, which is repeatedly described as being 'unto the praise of God's glory' (Eph. 1.6, 12, 14; Phil. 2.11) is equally 'unto our glory' (1 Cor. 2.7): for Christians *are* 'the glory of Christ' (2 Cor. 8.23; *cf.* 1 Thess. 2.12; 2 Thess. 1.10, 12; 2.14; Eph. 1.18; Col. 1.27).

The completion of this transformation must wait upon the day of the *Parousia* (1 Cor. 15.52; Rom. 8.19; Phil. 3.20), yes, even for those who have the firstfruits of the Spirit (Rom. 8.23). Nevertheless, as Christians, we have in this 'Holy Spirit of promise' 'an earnest of our inheritance, unto the redemption of God's own possession' (Eph. 1.13 f). Because of our incorporation into Christ the new solidarity is continually being built up within us. The condition of being 'conformed' bodily (σύμμορφον) to the body of His glory (Phil. 3.21; *cf.* Rom. 8.29) is only the end of the process, begun at baptism, whereby Christ is being 'formed'

---

[1] There is, of course, nothing automatic about baptism. It is 'faith working through love' that 'availeth' (Gal. 5.6). The Body is built up and cemented not by baptism but by love (Eph. 4.16; Col. 3.14 f). Baptism places a man within the sphere where this grace is operative, but he may fall away, with terrible consequences to the body (1 Cor. 10.1-12).

[2] *I.e.*, 'a living being'. ψυχή is not opposed to σῶμα but translates *nephesh* of Gen. 2.7, which designates the body as animated. *Cf.* H. Wheeler Robinson: 'It is quite misleading to translate the phrase *nephesh hayyah* by "a living soul", as our English versions do, so putting the emphasis where a Greek, but not a Hebrew, would have done' (*Inspiration and Revelation in the Old Testament*, 70).

within us (μορφώθη, Gal. 4.19). 'Our inward man *is being renewed* day by day', and 'our light affliction . . . *worketh* (now, not merely hereafter: κατεργάζεται, as in 2 Cor. 5.5) for us more and more exceedingly an eternal weight of glory' (2 Cor. 4.16 f). 'We all, with unveiled face reflecting as a mirror the glory of the Lord, *are being transformed* (μεταμορφούμεθα) into the same image from glory to glory, even as from the Lord Spirit' (2 Cor. 3.18). The final 'change' may be revealed 'in a moment, in the twinkling of an eye, at the last trump' (1 Cor. 15.52); but that is because the old solidarity will fall away in a flash, to lay bare how already all things in Christ 'are become new' (2 Cor. 5.17).

The habit of treating 1 Cor. 15 in isolation from the rest of Paul's writing has tended to obscure its connection with the very much larger number of passages which depict this gradual transformation and glorification of the body from baptism onwards. The result is that the final change has become mistakenly conceived as quasi-magical and unrelated to anything that has gone before.

The dissociation of this chapter from Paul's whole doctrine of the Body of Christ has also led to the supposition that Paul thought of the resurrection of the body in a purely individualistic manner. But this is quite untrue even of 1 Cor. 15. It is instructive to notice how he refuses to answer the question in the individual form in which his imaginary objector raises it (v. 35). Beginning at once in v. 36, he propounds his teaching throughout in abstract and collective terms, and concludes (vv. 42-4): 'What is sown is mortal, what rises is immortal . . .' (Moffatt), and, later, 'this corruptible (neuter) must put on incorruption, and this mortal must put on immortality' (vv. 53 f). It is hardly necessary to say that 'the first Adam' and 'the last Adam', 'the first man' and 'the last man' (vv. 45, 47) are for him essentially representative and corporate figures.

When this chapter is set in its proper context of the whole Pauline theology, it becomes quite impossible to think of the resurrection hope in terms of the individual unit. The carrier of the glory (ἔνδοξον, literally, 'a thing full of glory') is not the

individual but *the Church* (Eph. 5.27). The Church has been
rendered capable of this by baptism, 'the general baptism for all
men . . . at Golgotha' (O. Cullmann, *Baptism in the New Testament*,
29), wherein Christ 'gave himself for it; that he might sanctify it
by the washing of water with the word' (Eph. 5.25 f).[1] The
powers of life and death have thus been released within the Body.
And, if the whole is to be interfused, they must operate not
simply within each cell as a closed system but between the members. There must be a constant reciprocity of giving and receiving
within the Body. Thus, says Paul, 'Death worketh in us, but life
in you' (2 Cor. 4.12); 'We live if ye stand fast in the Lord' (1 Thess.
3.8); 'My tribulations for you are your glory', *i.e.*, your eschatological perfection (Eph. 3.13; *cf.* 2 Cor. 1.6); 'We rejoice when
we are weak, and ye are strong: this we also pray for, even your
perfecting' (2 Cor. 13.9); 'We are your glorying, even as ye also
are ours, in the day of our Lord Jesus' (2 Cor. 1.14; *cf.* 1 Thess.
2.20).

And so the great work of redemption is carried forward, 'unto
the building up of the body of Christ: till we all attain to the
unity of the faith, and of the knowledge of the Son of God, unto
a fullgrown man, unto the measure of the stature of the fulness
of Christ: that we may . . . grow up in all things into him, which
is the head, even Christ; from whom all the body fitly framed and
knit together through that which every joint supplieth, according
to the working of each several part, maketh the increase of the
body to the building up of itself in love' (Eph. 4.12-16).

And as the Christian hope of resurrection is fundamentally
social, so it is inescapably historical. It is a resurrection, not from
the body, but of the body. The new creation is not a fresh start,
but the old made new—not a *νέα* but a *καινὴ κτίσις* (2 Cor. 5.17).
It is this very body of sin and death which, transformed, 'must
put on incorruption' (1 Cor. 15.54). The building up of the
Church is not the gathering of an elect group *out of* the body of

[1] The background of this passage is Jahweh's address to His bride in Ezek.
16.8-14. *Cf.* especially Eph. 5.26 with Ezek. 16.9 (LXX: καὶ ἔλουσά σε ἐν ὕδατι,
καὶ ἀπέπλυνα τὸ αἷμα σου ἀπὸ σοῦ, καὶ ἔχρισά σε ἐν ἐλαίῳ).

history, which is itself signed simply for destruction. It *is* the resurrection body of history itself, the world as its redemption has so far been made effective. 'The open consecration of a part marks the destiny of the whole' (B. F. Westcott, *The Victory of the Cross*, 51; quoted, A. R. Vidler, *The Theology of F. D. Maurice*, 73). The mass of human existence, for all its sin, its destructiveness, its determinisms, is still σῶμα: it is made for God. Though it may have become conformed to the σάρξ and its end, that is not its true constitution as it has been created and redeemed in Christ. The Church is at once the witness to the world of its true nature and the pledge and instrument of its destiny. Those incorporated by God into the Body of His Son are to be 'a kind of firstfruits of his creatures' (James 1.18). So Paul sees the redemption of the body begun in the eschatological community of the Spirit (Rom. 8.11) as the hope ultimately, not only of all men, but of 'the creation itself' (Rom. 8.21). It is '*into* the liberty of the glory of the children of God', into the resurrection mode of existence of those who even now can be described as 'glorified' (Rom. 8.30), that all things are finally to be brought. This day has not yet dawned. It waits upon 'the revealing', or unveiling, 'of the sons of God' (Rom. 8.19), which is the same as 'the revelation of the Lord Jesus', 'when he shall come to be glorified *in* his saints' (2 Thess. 1.7, 10). But then the Body of Christ will stand forth, not, as it is now, a world within a world, but as the one solidarity, the restoration of the original image of creation, 'where there cannot be Greek and Jew, circumcision and uncircumcision, barbarian, Scythian, bondman, freeman: but Christ is all, and in all' (Col. 3.10 f).

INDEX OF BIBLICAL REFERENCES

OLD TESTAMENT

Index of Biblical References

Index of Biblical References

INDEX OF NAMES